PATRICIA BROOKER grew up in Bow in East London, where she married husband Charlie and had five children. After working in various East End factories, she became landlady of The Rising Sun before moving to Essex and working as a newsagent and then dinner lady. She was catapulted to fame in ITV's *The Only Way is Essex*, where, as matriarch of the Wright clan, she quickly became one of the most popular characters. She has fourteen grandchildren and six great grandchildren.

Nanny Pat

Penny Sweets and Cobbled Streets

MY EAST END CHILDHOOD

PAN BOOKS

First published 2012 by Pan Books
an imprint of Pan Macmillan, a division of Macmillan Publishers Limited
Pan Macmillan, 20 New Wharf Road, London N1 9RR
Basingstoke and Oxford
Associated companies throughout the world
www.panmacmillan.com

ISBN 978-1-4472-1875-3 PB
ISBN 978-1-4472-2561-4 SPL

1 3 5 7 9 8 6 4 2

A CIP catalogue record for this book is available from the British Library.

Maps by HL Studios, Witney, Oxon
Typeset by Ellipsis Digital Limited, Glasgow
Printed and bound by CPI Group (UK) Ltd, Croydon CR0 4YY

PROLOGUE

I was seventy-five years old the first time someone asked for my autograph.

Fame was not something I went looking for, nor was it something I ever expected. But somehow it happened to little ol' me! So at the age when most people are retiring, and heading off to their caravans by the sea to watch the world go by in peace, I was whizzing about here, there and everywhere, from filming for *The Only Way is Essex*, to TV interview, to launch party.

I got pulled into the show by chance, when my grandson Mark Wright started filming, and I had a bit of a cameo when I called round his flat with some home-made food for him. I felt daft, but it was just a laugh, until my weekly food drops for him, especially the sausage plaits, suddenly got popular with the *TOWIE* audience. Then before I knew it, my TV career took off.

I am sure if my husband Charlie was still here, he'd be saying to me, 'What the bleedin' hell you doing, you daft woman?!', but I tell you what, exhausting though it has been, I've loved (mostly) every minute of it.

But this book is not about any of that really. It is about the first half of my life, a normal childhood, far away from anything I am living now. My life growing up and falling in love in the East End of London – Devons Road and Canning Town to be exact.

It's about a bit of London and a way of life that still exists on some levels, but that has completely disappeared on another. What you'll probably see as you read, is that that's awful when it comes to some things – and a right blessing when it comes to others!

There are some characters and ways of behaving that were so true to the old East End, especially around the time of the war, that have sadly, gone now for ever. But that's why I am writing this book. I want to give people a glimpse of a piece of London that to me just seems normal, but one I know, from talking to my kids and grandkids seems completely strange yet fascinating to other people.

So whether you will be seeing all this through new eyes, or you are an East End old-timer and are reading this for the memories, please do this the proper way. By that I mean you should be settled back by now, with a

For my family

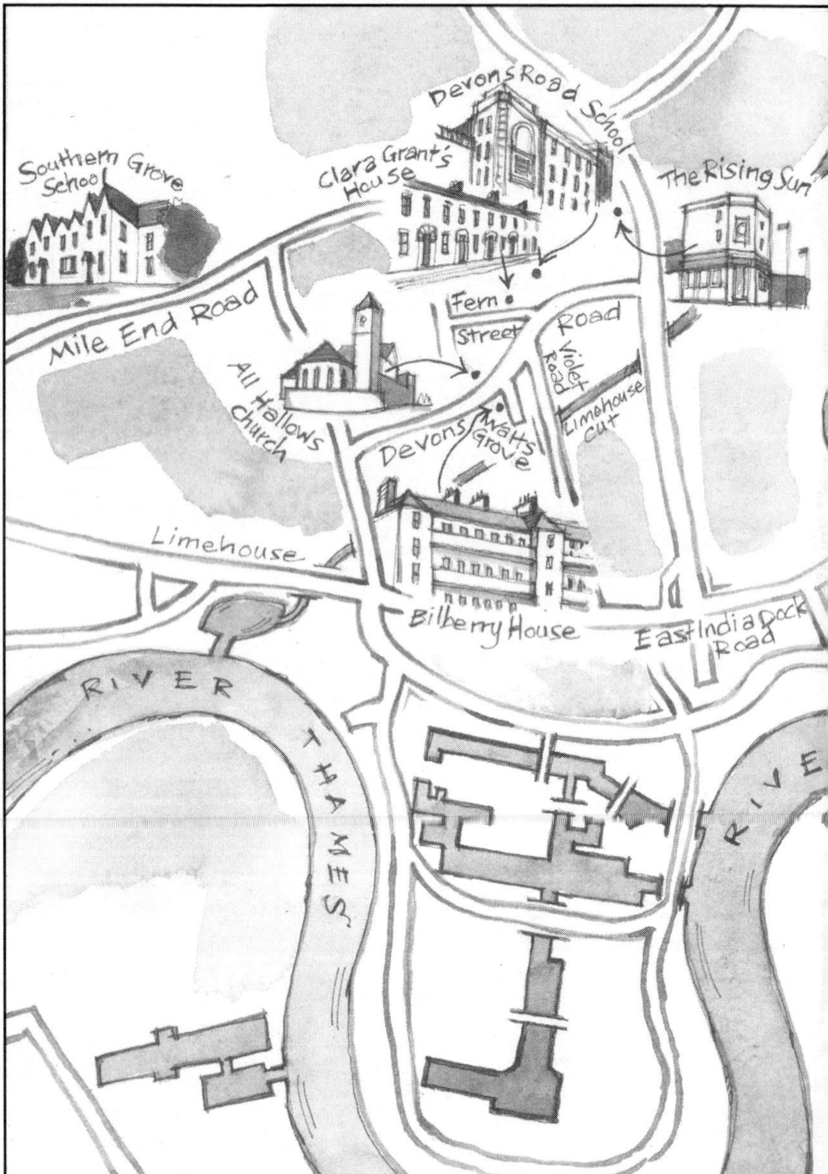

Devons Road School
Southern Grove School
Clara Grant's House
The Rising Sun
Mile End Road
Fern Street
Road
Violet Road
All Hallows Church
Limehouse Cut
Devons
Watts Grove
Limehouse
Bilberry House
East India Dock Road
RIVER THAMES
RIVE

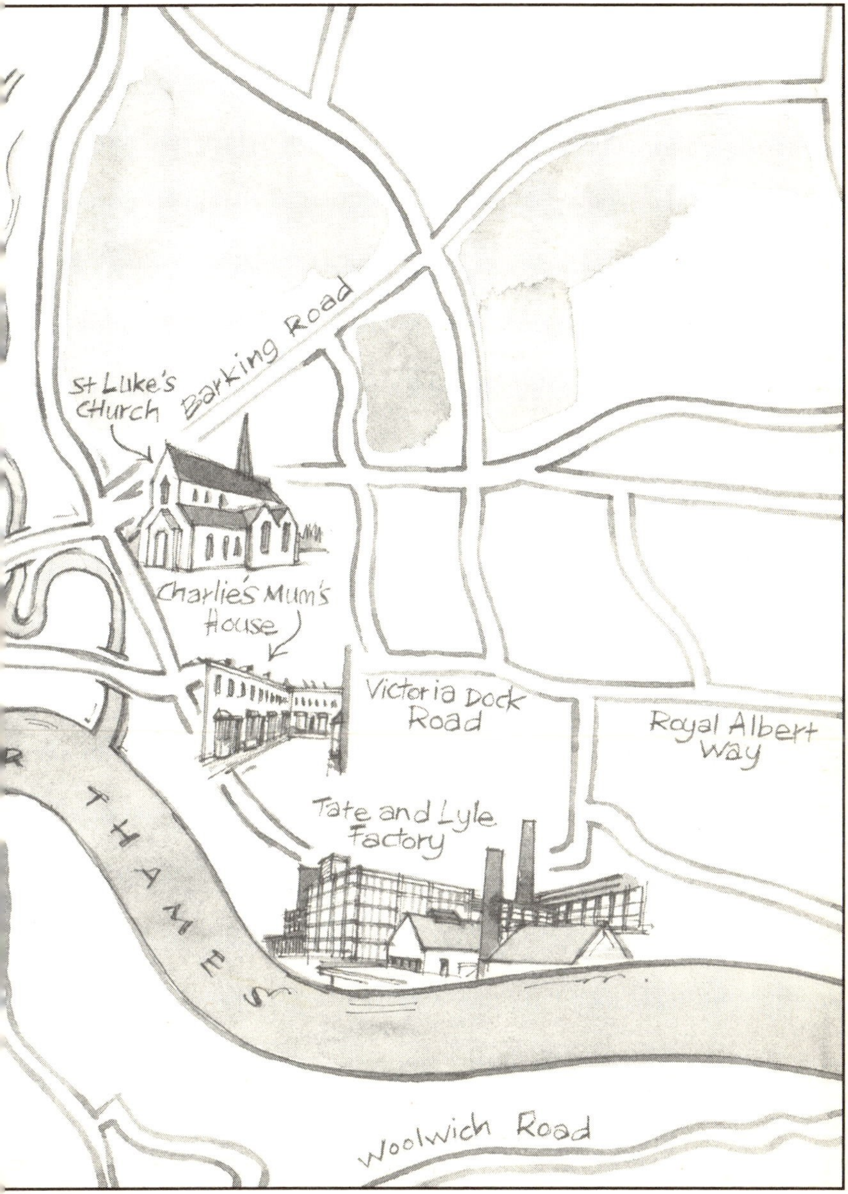
Barking Road
St Luke's Church
Charlie's Mum's House
Victoria Dock Road
Royal Albert Way
Tate and Lyle Factory
THAMES
Woolwich Road

CONTENTS

plateful of jellied eels on your lap, a takeaway pint from the local pub, and the wireless crackling away next to you . . .

ONE
The Ol' Bow Bells

When I was a little 'un, you didn't talk to your parents. Least not about anything outside of the situation you were in at that time, or the life you were living then and there. So it was all about school, work, food, housework, and . . . well, really, that was it.

'Come on, get yourself ready for school,' Mum would say. Or, 'Move it, get cleaned and the table set for dinner.' Then, 'Hurry up, get yourself ready for bed.' It definitely wasn't the thing to sit and talk about stuff like the past, or feelings, or anything like that.

Besides that, my mum and dad were always working, so even if you wanted to, you didn't get a chance to sit down and exchange words about events that didn't have anything to do with your day-to-day needs. My mum would go to work of a morning, and I just had to go to school. Then after school, depending on what shifts she was working, I would go home, or stay with an auntie until she had finished, then in the evening there wasn't much time together before bed. I was young then, of course, while she was still alive.

So now you can see why, although a lot of people start their memoirs with a chapter on their parents', even their grandparents' lives before they were born themselves, well, if I did it, with the little I know, it'd be a pretty sorry looking chapter.

Although there is one thing about my mum's family that I do know and think is worth a mention. Her surname before she married my dad was Chipperfield, and she was part of the family who ran Chipperfield Circus, which is that world-famous circus you might have heard of.

She and her sister Violet, who was about four years older and her only sister, came from the circus family. I don't know if Mum ever actually had to perform – I like to think she might have, though. Trapeze artist, shot out of a cannon, a horseback ballerina . . . I'd settle for her having done any of it. We used to go and watch that circus when we were young and it was in town. They would set up every year on Blackheath, and we went along a couple of times as a family. It was quite a way from Devons Road – about five or six miles – and we didn't have a car then, but we'd get the bus. It was a great day out, and a really big deal for me and my brother Tommy. We'd be talking about it for weeks afterwards.

Chipperfield Circus still exists today, but they have had to stop using animals. Then, though, it was full of tigers and elephants and zebras, as well as the clowns and trapeze artists and that. It was amazing to go to as a kid. Quite another world. Maybe I had some circus blood in me, for I'd sometimes watch them and think how I'd quite like to be living their life!

It's one of my regrets that I didn't ever take the time to ask my mum about all of that, then again I don't suppose she'd have wanted to talk about it. The only time she mentioned it she went quiet after, and that was the end of it.

My dad's family meantime were all East End through and through, and had been running the fish trade in the area for years. He was one of thirteen children, not to mention all his cousins and other relatives, so wherever you went in the area you were sure to bump into a Spicer!

So anyway, Winifred Chipperfield – known to her friends as Win – and Thomas John Spicer – known as Tom – were both born around 1912. They met and fell in love and married in their late teens.

My dad was a tall, handsome man with mousey brown hair, while my mum was slim and quiet, and really lovely looking.

They started their married life in a flat in Watts Grove, near Devons Road in Bow, and hadn't been married long when they decided to start a family. Along came their first screaming bundle – my brother – in 1931. In true East End tradition, he was named after my dad, although to tell the difference between Thomas senior and junior my dad's name was shortened to Tom, while we mostly called my brother Tommy.

Then just as my mum was about to send him off to school and get some peace to herself again during the day, I came along four and a half years later, on 21 November 1935. I've no idea what time of day and get amazed when people ask me – funnily enough I don't remember, and that kind of sentimental thinking didn't really exist then, so it wasn't written in a baby book for me to pore over years later or anything. You were just more than happy the baby was born healthy, and that the mother had survived the birth.

I was born in hospital, St Andrew's Hospital in Bromley-by Bow to be precise. Not that it's there anymore, it's been knocked down and modern housing has been built where it was. A lot of the hospitals have been knocked down in East London – I could list off plenty of others that used to be around. I don't understand why myself. Surely the more people there are, the more hospitals you need, but it seems to be going in reverse!

Anyway, from what I have been told, that definitely makes me a proper cockney as it's within earshot of the ol' Bow Bells at St Mary-le-Bow church in the city, although I'm sure that must be true for most of the East End. Everyone who comes from the East End likes to consider themselves cockney – it's kind of the ultimate Londoner title!

Now my parents must have been a bit shocked when I popped out 'cause I had a shock of ginger hair – and they both have brown hair! But two of my dad's brothers were right ginger, so I guess it came from his side of the family. No milkman-style scandal or anything like that there, thank you very much, despite the on-going jokes.

Anyway, my mum and dad took me home from hospital to the flat, number 12 Bilberry House. I can remember that address like anything, as it became my home for the next twenty years.

Bow is in the heart of the East End of London, just north of the Thames River. At that time it was an area mostly made up of council houses and flats, mixed in amongst factories. It was quite built up, with not many green areas – it was more about industry back then.

Our flat was off a road called Devons Road, which was where most of the local shops were. It was a main road, but there was never much traffic – you didn't get many cars around there in them days.

To get to our flat you came off Devons Road into a cobbled street called Watts Grove. Looking back, I wonder why they bothered with cobbles, but it seemed like loads of the roads were done that way. They weren't always so easy to walk on, though, and you were forever twisting your ankle. I remember running up Watts Grove when I was late for school and nearly taking a fall dozens of times. Running and cobbles are never a good combination. But that was a common way for the roads to be done in them days, so you got kind of used to it. Now cobbles are just for decoration really, aren't they?

Our flat was on the second floor of a four-storey block, built in the 1920s or 30s. To get to it you went up some stairs and along a balcony walkway – the landing, as we always used to call it. Our flat was the one at the end, in the corner. It's years since I've been there, but I'd have no problem finding it at all now.

We had a front door that I suppose had a lock on it, not that we ever used it – you just didn't get people breaking into each other's houses then. And the reality was there was nothing in there worth stealing anyway.

So you'd go through the door, and there was a little bit of a passageway. Then there was a front room, a kitchen, a bigger bedroom for my parents, and a smaller bedroom with two little single beds in it that me and my brother shared, until he left. Then we got rid of one bed, and I had it all to myself. Bliss! Oh, and there was a toilet – a tiny little room that just about fitted a toilet and a small circular wash basin. All the rooms were small, and basic, I suppose you'd say, but my mum had done her best to make it homely and nice. Besides, you didn't have anything like the amount of furniture or belongings what you do today. So like we hardly needed many wardrobes 'cause we hardly owned any clothes, and what we had we were busy looking after and mending.

The front room was where we spent most of our time. It was where the fireplace was, so in the winter it was the only place you wanted to be. And there was a settee and you would go in there to listen to the radio or do needlework, or it was where my dad would bring his friends.

My mum was mostly found in the kitchen, which was also the bathroom – sounds strange today, but that's often how it was back then – the bath was in here so it could be by the boiler to get hot water. But 'cause there wasn't much space, it also had to double up as something else, so had a wooden top you pulled down over it to turn it into the kitchen table. All very practical, I can tell you!

Unlike the hospital, the flats are still there today, but they've changed a lot. All modernized and with baths in the bathroom and everything.

As for our block of flats, they were all council-owned flats 'cause no one round our area would have been rich enough to own their own place. But it was a great selection of people who lived in them. I think I liked all of them mostly, except one scary old lady who lived in the building opposite. She used to sit and look out the window all the time and bang on the window for no reason. So we'd pull faces at her and run off. I think we decided she was a witch!

Apart from her, maybe it was the fact that people weren't well off, or maybe it was just how things were in them days, but it was a really friendly area. I know it sounds like a stereotype, but everyone really did know each other, and helped each other out when they could. Everybody knew everybody's business, partly out of nosiness, of course, but mostly 'cause they were looking out for each other.

Also people hardly ever moved. Why would you? So people had lived in the same flat all their lives, and people were next to others they had grown up with. Friends were as much your family as your family was, half the time. And while it was clear who your parents were, everyone chipped in with looking after each other's children where they could – they were more like aunts and uncles than neighbours, and that's exactly what they ended up being called.

So I had a lot of women I called 'Auntie', but they weren't actually aunties in the sense that they were related to me by blood. At least some of them were, and some of them may have been, but mostly it was just a term we used for any woman we were talking to or about. It meant half the time I didn't even know people's actual Christian names! They were just 'Auntie over the road' or 'Auntie in number twenty-one' and somehow people knew who you were talking about. It might sound odd now, but it was totally normal then.

It was the same when you were talking about men, they were always 'Uncle' and their kids were mostly called my cousins.

To people who didn't live in that time and place I know it sounds strange. I don't think my grandkids can believe that I didn't know who were my blood relatives and who were not, but in a way I don't suppose it really mattered. The community had an overall family feel.

So I suppose because of that, no one kept themselves separate. Everybody would be constantly going between homes and popping in for a gossip, or to swap some tips, or to keep an eye on someone's kids, or just to be plain nosey.

My best friend from when I was as small as I can remember was a girl called Winnie Armitage. She lived in our flats on the next landing and we were pretty much always together. We'd walk to and from school together, we were in the same class, and we played together.

She was from a great big family – there were thirteen children in her family. Can you imagine that?! They had two flats to share as a family, and I remember her parents lived in one with half the kids, and her grandma in the other with the rest of the children, and they both sort of oversaw running both flats. Big families were pretty common, but this one was big even by those days' standards. But it didn't seem to do them any harm. They were well brought-up kids.

She had a sister a couple of years older than us, called Gracie. She was a nice girl too, and was the oldest of the thirteen kids, so knew a lot about the ways of the world. It seemed like the age gap between us was much bigger than two years, and she taught me a few things as I was growing up.

The rent we paid on our flat was 12 shillings and 6 pence a week, which seemed a lot of money at the time. A man from the council used to come around and knock on the door every Monday to collect it. You'd see people pulling their curtains and not answering the door if they didn't have the money. But my mum and dad must have been good at keeping the rent aside 'cause I always remember them paying on time.

The majority of the area was poor, but that doesn't

mean anything really – no one was rich in them days as far as I could see, least not in East London, and definitely no one I came across.

You never had expensive toys, or holidays, or cars parked up outside your door or anything like that. Cars could just be borrowed from the odd well-off person for special occasions like weddings or funerals. And you earned your way in life. Sitting around was never an option. If you were out of work you swept the roads to get a couple of coppers if that's what it took. People weren't too proud in them days – it was a fool who sat home rather than getting out and providing for his family. I guess that's where the saying 'working class' came from, and we were a working-class family, no doubt about that. My parents were real hard-working people. So hard working, in fact, that I don't remember seeing much of my dad for the first nine years of my life – because he was never around. Then he was called up to serve in the Navy during the Second World War. I'm not sure that he liked it 'cause it wasn't as if he was there out of choice, I don't suppose. Either way, he was away most of the time for as much as I can remember of my early years.

As for my mum, it seemed like she was always working. My early memories of her revolve around her leaving for work. She worked five days a week, and as many hours as she could, in some factory or another.

The main job I remember her doing was in a factory called Morton's over at Millwall. Morton's was a great big food-production factory. They did lots of canned food, jams, tea, meat . . . anything and everything, as far as I could tell. Then much of it was put on to the ships and taken to other countries from the nearby Royal Victoria Dock. But more importantly, as far as I was concerned, they made sweets! Everything from candied fruit to boiled sweets, and luckily for me, that was where my mum's job was.

It was like temptation was being put in front of the workers every day, and my crafty mum soon found a way to give in to that temptation without getting in trouble, thanks to her trusty turban!

A turban was what we called a scarf that she would wear over her head. It was made of cotton. To do it, she'd fold a scarf into a triangle by putting two of the corners together, put it over her head with the point of the triangle dangling over her nose – I always remember she'd hold it in her teeth to keep it there. Then she'd loop the other two corners down under her neck and back up to the top and tie it in a bow. Then the dangling bit of the triangle would be tucked back and over and there you go, it was all neat and finished, very simple to do. My mum could do her turban quick as a jiffy of a morning, mostly while she was trying to do ten other jobs as well.

If you remember any of the typical images of women from the forties with a scarf on their head, such as one of those land army girls in dungarees, no doubt it will be a turban they are wearing. They were all the fashion then, but the original reasons for it were about practicality. First, of course, it was to keep your hair out of the way so you wouldn't have to spend time styling it in the morning. It was just hidden. If you did want to style it, though, you'd put your hair in rollers at night, and then put the scarf over it to keep it in place, and sleep that way. It also acted as a good hair protector in the rain – we had no need for brollies in them days, the turbans made sure our hair stayed dry. But it soon turned out there was a much better use for it, as my mum discovered – smuggling sweets out of the factory and home to us!

Each day as they clocked out and left the factory, the workers would be searched to check that they hadn't taken anything. Mum was so lovely looking, and slim and quiet and innocent, that I am sure they didn't look too closely with her. Either way, they might have searched all her pockets and wherever else, but they never thought to check inside my clever mum's turban. At some point near the end of each day, a few of these little sweets would be slipped up the side of her turban and underneath it when no one was looking. Then she'd bring these sweets home and put them into this bowl in a cupboard in the sideboard, and now and again it would be pulled out as a treat for us all. It doubled our excitement each day at seeing her get home, especially me, as I have always had quite a sweet tooth! Least I have ever since then, so maybe she caused it!

Everyone jokes that I am always guaranteed to have a handful of sweets in my bag, or in my pocket, just to keep me going through the day, or to give to the kids. And I think it started back with my mum. Liquorice, lemon sherbets, white mice, rhubarb and custards . . . I don't even have a set favourite – I like every sweet going! I even have a whole drawer at home just for sweets. How times have changed, even if my taste buds haven't!

It was harder when Mum wasn't working in the factory anymore, though, 'cause you wouldn't really ever be able to go and buy sweets. That would have been seen as too much of a luxury, to go and spend money in a sweet shop. It's not like today when people are buying them every day. There was one shop in Devons Road, on the corner of Blackthorn Street, called Peter's. It used to have great jars of sweets that I'd eye up each time I walked past. And on the very rare occasion that I had a spare copper or was given a present of a penny, I'd go in and treat myself to whatever sweet I'd been dreaming of recently.

As for Morton's factory, I'm not sure what happened to it, but it has long gone – from what I remember it must be buried somewhere under the towers of Canary Wharf . . . Yep, the East End has moved on a lot in recent years.

TWO

Evacuation

The war against Germany began on 1 September 1939 when I was three, nearly four. So not surprisingly I don't remember it starting. My parents would have heard the announcement on the radio – the same way they got most of their information throughout the war – and now, as an adult, I wonder what must have gone through their minds. Older people always used to talk about the First World War, and how terrible that was, so the idea that we were about to go through something similar again – well, I can only imagine it must have been awful.

But despite the announcement, not a lot happened at the start. There was no bombing in Britain, or any signs that we were at war, apart from what was said on the radio. Or this is how I later understood it from what people have told me.

My own earliest memory of anything to do with the

war is being fitted with a gas mask. We were called over to the local church for a meeting. My church was All Hallows church, on Blackthorn Street in Bow, and it was a big part of my life. Not 'cause I am deeply religious or anything, but more for the social side of it. I'm not a well-known churchgoer these days, except maybe at Christmas or special occasions, but I still think religion is a good thing, and has a part to play in the world.

Back then I went more 'cause church was central to everyone's lives, whether they were particularly religious minded or not, much more than it is today. So meetings were held there, as well as social gatherings and the likes, and 'specially during the war, they were central to helping people out and keeping people them informed about what was going on.

The church was just minutes from my house. You'd go to the end of the street, cross the main road, and it was in the road opposite. It is still there today, although it has changed a lot since.

Anyway, that day, gas masks were handed round and I remember someone trying them on me and Tommy, and showing our mum what to do with them. It seemed more of a game to me than anything – I had no idea at the time that this was seen by everyone as possibly the only thing that could save us if those poison gas bombs were dropped on us. Everyone worried about that a lot, as so many people had been killed or injured by poison gas in the First World War. The main fear was that mustard gas would be dropped on us as the effects of that sounded horrible. People always said if they added that to the bombs dropping on London it would be devastating. It has no smell so you don't even know if it is in the air. Then there was tear gas and chlorine to worry about.

They were funny things, gas masks. I remember mine was this kind of weird red rubber, with big eyes in it, and a bit like a tin can in the mask that went over your mouth which was supposed to get rid of any poisons if gas dropped. I think it had charcoal or something in it, which would soak up the gas. There were strings that held it in place behind your head, and the rest of the time you wore it round your neck, dangling on one of the strings. Bleedin' annoying a lot of the time!

The mask I was given that day became my own personal mask for the rest of the war. You were supposed to have it with you all the time, in case you needed it. So I would take it with me wherever I went – when I was evacuated, when I went to school, when I went running to the bunkers to hide from the sirens. Sometimes you would leave it somewhere, and forget about it, then panic would kick in and you'd realize you didn't have it and needed to find it. Luckily, although I did put it on on a lot of occasions, I never needed it for an actual gas attack. But it helped me breathe through dust and smoke and the like at times, after bombs had dropped. And as the war continued people got lazier about keeping their masks nearby, as they soon realized gas attacks didn't seem to be happening.

But anyway, apart from the presence of the mask, I think my life continued pretty much the same for a few months, until one day at the start of 1940.

My memory on dates around this time is obviously very vague – as you can imagine at four years old, what day, month, or even year it is, is pretty meaningless to you. But anyhow, matching up my memories in as much of a jigsaw as I can, I reckon on it being about February time of that year, when one day Mum told me and Tommy we had to go over to the church for another meeting. So she took mine and my brother's hands and we walked over again. When we got there the vicar was telling everyone what was going on. I wasn't listening or understanding very much, all I did get was that us kids were about to be sent off on a nice trip to the countryside, and we should be excited about it! So of course we were.

Then I think we had a couple of days to prepare before we left. This was, of course, us being evacuated. The government had decided that it would be a good idea for children in all the big cities that were at risk of being bombed to move to the countryside where it was supposed to be safer. No one had to, but it was recommended, and I think most people did it.

I'm sure it must have been horrible for my mum, sending her kids off and not even knowing where they were going or who they'd be staying with, but she put a brave face on it. I don't remember her getting upset, at least not in front of us – I'm sure she saved it until she was in private. She was a strong lady, my mum, and I remember her explaining again before we left.

'Now don't forget,' Mum said, smiling at me. 'You're just going away on holiday 'cause of this war business. You're going to have such a nice time in the country. Now make sure you're a good girl and mind what Tommy and the people who will look after you tell you to do.'

And that was it. I was so young I don't think I realized what was happening, and at first I think me and Tommy were excited 'cause we were going on holiday, and we didn't know any better. Even though, at almost nine, he was a fair bit older than me, I don't think Tommy understood the concept of war much better than I did.

I'd never been on holiday, but I liked the sound of it, and we were told we'd be going to stay in a lovely big house. We had always lived in a flat so didn't know what a house was like, or what it was to have a garden with trees – we had none of that, so it was exciting. That was all we were focused on, I suppose. It was good how it was built up to us kids like really.

Then the next thing I knew I was getting on a coach at the church. Although I was leaving home without my parents, I honestly don't think I gave it a second thought as there was so much to distract me. Which, I suppose, is exactly how they wanted it! Besides I had my brother with me, so it wasn't all totally alien, as well as several adults who herded us all about the place. I don't know who they were, volunteers perhaps.

The coach took us to a train station somewhere in London. No one told me which one, but I have a feeling it was King's Cross. When I have seen pictures of the station from back then, it looks the most familiar.

So there I was with a little tiny brown suitcase, my best pinny and coat, and a little red beret – my best outfit, I suppose, looking back, as my mum must have realized a good first impression at the other end could only have helped. Oh, and obviously I had my gas mask round my neck. No forgetting about that! And I had a white label tied around my wrist, with my name and address written on it, in case I got lost. Other kids had them tied around a button on their coat, but wherever they were fixed, every kid had a label. I remember studying the label, and thinking we were like parcels, being sent off as presents and that hopefully the person getting us would be pleased!

Looking back, I think Tommy quite liked his role of being in charge of me, and kept putting a protective arm around me. 'This way. Keep up. Nearly there.' And all that.

Sometimes when I see old-fashioned films or TV shows they show footage from that time, and I wonder to myself if I am one of the children on it, because we didn't know whether it was being filmed. And it certainly looks like the memory I have in my mind. I remember this huge place filled with smoky air and lots of people all moving quickly. It was noisy too – it was steam trains in them days and they do make a lot of noise chugging along. I called them choo choos back then 'cause of the noise. Then they were forever pulling their whistles, to let people know they were coming or going. Yes, King's Cross, if that was it, was a noisy place!

Anyway, I had never been on a train before in my life, so again it was another thing making me excited about this trip rather than scared.

The adults travelling with us took us along a platform, all of us walking together like, and I was holding my brother's hand, looking round me.

'Boys this way! Girls that way!' someone shouted out.

Suddenly Tommy and me were separated. Before I knew it they took the boys off on a different train. I'm sure I was sad to see my brother go, but I didn't have time to think about it because we were hurried on to our own train. I was still focused on my own big adventure!

We were all sat in carriages, trying to wriggle into our places, with the bigger children getting all bossy and 'move up there' and the likes. I think we might have had the whole train to ourselves. I suppose it was put on especially to transport us all. Then we were off! I thought it was brilliant, sitting on the seat with my legs swinging, not even long enough to touch the floor, and the sound of the steam puffing away outside, while countryside like I'd never seen shot past the window. You have to remember up until this point the furthest I had been was literally a few streets from my home. My life until now had been lived within about a two-square mile radius of Bilberry House. Flat, church, shops – that in all seriousness was about the extent of life as I knew it.

Eventually we pulled up at our destination – wherever that may have been. I know this sounds awful, but to this day I still don't know where it was. Although, to be honest, at that age it would have meant nothing to me anyway. I have a vague idea it was in Derbyshire – I remember my dad mentioning that at some point years later. But do you know, there is no official national record to tell you? Can you imagine that happening these days, kids all shipped off to different parts of the country, and no one actually makes a big list of who is where? It seems crazy now. But I suppose it all happened in such a rush, it was a case of making do. Put your trust in strangers, or stay in London and risk getting blown up. That was the choice.

Anyhow, when we got out of the train at the station, pulling our little cases with us – and gas masks round our necks still, of course – we were told to stand in a line. There were other children there by then, including boys, so I guess they had come from another city too. Then this group of adults, mostly women, came over and picked which children they wanted.

What was happening was they were mums who had agreed to put up children in their homes – they had volunteered to be our new foster mums or whatever they were called – and they were looking at us, and would point and choose who they wanted. 'I'll have that one but I won't have that one', or 'I'll have her but not them,' that kind of thing. I remember that bit happening clearly, people picking you out. I suppose they all had a set idea of who they could look after, like if you owned a farm, you wanted a big boy who could help out and earn his keep, rather than a small young girl. I think there were just so many children to sort out, they couldn't think of a better way to do it, you know?

I remember feeling anxious that I wouldn't get picked, and might not get the holiday I had been promised or, worse still, I'd just be left standing on the platform alone. But I got picked out by a lady quite quickly – my mum's choice of best clothes paid off – along with four or five other children, including a couple of girls from my block of flats back home. But they were older and I don't really remember them well.

Then we were taken back to her house, all of us trailing along the road behind her in a line, not having a clue what we were doing really. But, ooh, when we got there we were pleased 'cause what a nice house she had. It was like a big old farmhouse and it was right in the countryside with real animals and trees and everything.

I shared a room with three or four other kids. In fact, I shared a bed with them too. We went top and bottom, as it was called. Top and tail, or head to feet, call it what you like, but basically it meant a couple of you with your head at each end, all in the same bed. We were only little so it was fine. And it was only girls in the same bed, of course, boys were in a different room.

I don't remember the name of the lady who took me in – maybe I was never told it. And even if I did know her first name, I would never ever have used it. As with the way I called people in London, to me she was an auntie. So if I wanted her attention I would just say 'Auntie', and tug on her skirt or coat. There weren't so many grown-ups around there, you didn't get a group of women around the house, so there was never confusion over who I was talking to or about.

But, oh, the animals she had, they were my favourite bit of being an evacuee – cows, chickens, rabbits in this great big pen, and dogs. I liked the dogs, they were good ones – they were playful, and would never have gone for you, unless you tormented them and asked for it! We had to look after the animals, and I remember one of the hardest tasks was getting the eggs. They were like gold dust at the time, so if you dropped an egg, that was it! You were in real trouble, and got a telling-off, and most likely had to miss out on an egg next time. So we used to carry them like they were awful precious . . .

Then you had to do a bit of housework, and I remember there were a couple of boys who would be sent to cut down trees and drag them back, because there was an open fire and they had to put the logs on it to get that going.

But that was it really, I'd mostly be left on my own to play. Some of the older kids went to school, but I wasn't old enough, so I stayed home. And actually I think a lot of the kids didn't bother with school, even if they were old enough, because it wasn't really forced on you. In fact, from what I could understand, often your foster parents, as they got called, preferred you to be useful in the home. It was weird really, but at that time school and learning just wasn't a priority. I suppose when you have something so huge as the war going on, life becomes more about survival and the basics. Knowing the capital of America, or what happened in England five hundred years ago, didn't seem relevant to the life you were living.

As for what I wore, I just had the clothes what I had brought up in my little case, which was probably just a second pinny, pair of knickers, a vest and a cardigan or something. Plus, I suppose, my toothbrush, facecloth and a comb. I don't remember being given anything new. I suppose people just wore what they had, and if they needed to, washed it out overnight.

I got on fine with the other kids, but I was the youngest, so they didn't bother with me too much. They had their own games and things they were doing. Most of the time I was only too pleased if any of them even spoke to me! I suppose I was a bit lonely, but I didn't think about it too much, and got used to playing by myself. The woman had a daughter of her own, though, who I loved spending time with. I can't remember her name, but she was lovely that one, really lovely. She was about fourteen although she looked older, and she was probably more like my replacement mum when I was up there than her mum was. It sticks in my mind that her mum was alright, but I wasn't so taken with her. Her daughter, though, yep, lovely.

I remember the mum would tell you off if you did something wrong, and her tellings off were pretty strong. She really stood her ground, 'don't do this, don't do that, don't let me see you doing so and so'. And in them days you took notice and you wouldn't do it. You say that to kids now and they would just go and do it anyway. I suppose she had quite a lot to contend with, having all these extra kids in her house, but still, her strictness scared me a bit. She was a lot tougher than my mum, who could be quite brisk, but who mostly quietly talked you round to something, rather than yelling.

One time the mum cut all my hair off, and I cried and cried and cried. I had lovely long curly hair, and I used to have it nice, with a ribbon bow in it. But I think I must have scratched my head or something, and she went 'fleas, scrub her head, cut her hair off!' and someone did. All my lovely hair was cut into this short bob. I was so upset. I'm sure I didn't have fleas at all – it was more that she couldn't be bothered brushing it.

I remember other children coming to join the house afterwards from other places, but they never made that much of an impression on me. We were quite a busy household at one point, but I did keep to myself. I was quite a lone kid at that time, I'm not sure whether from choice or not. But I mostly remember playing on my own, and doing my own thing exploring around the garden and farm. This kind of independence was completely new to me, so I was actually rather pleased with it. And the weather was good. I think I was there through the spring and then into the summer, as I spent most of my time outdoors. It was probably pretty good for me as a city kid really, to get all that country air.

I think I was quite happy as an evacuee, but it was weird. And it's an experience and way of living that's hard to explain to people today.

I can't say I missed my dad, as I didn't see him much back home anyway. He was always away and backwards and forwards, even when he did come home for a week or two. But I missed having Tommy around, it was strange not to see him. And as for my mum, well, obviously, yeah, I missed my mum badly. I thought of her night after night. I used to lie there and wish I was at home with my mum. But you didn't show it much there like, you know. Whereas in this day and age you would have cried and complained, 'oh, where's my mum, can you find my mum', and everyone would run and make sure you were comforted, back then they wouldn't have taken much notice. So if you cried, as I did, it was quietly to yourself in bed, when you hoped no one else would realize what you were doing.

And it wasn't like you could call home 'cause we never had phones then, and I couldn't read or write, so letters weren't an option. Nowadays kids would be talking to their parents every day on mobile phones, or computers or the likes.

No one gave you any idea how long you were to be there for. Though I don't suppose the adults knew themselves. It was all just very open ended.

I don't remember too much conversation about the war neither. I guess as I was so young they didn't discuss it with me, or if it was mentioned, maybe I took no notice. As I learned later, the war around this time was being called 'the phoney war' because no one was actually doing much fighting, at least not that affected civilians in the UK. So maybe there wasn't much for people to talk about. Although I do remember how sometimes the woman running the house or friends of hers used to tell us 'bombs are going to drop in London, but they don't bomb here, so we'll all be safe'.

Luckily for me I was too young to think what this would mean for my mum, and that she might be in danger. I don't think I really even understood what a bomb was at this point, which is lucky 'cause I would have been scared stiff by the stuff they said. 'They will bomb in the East End and that is where you have all come from, you London kids.' That is what they always called us, 'the London kids'.

It was nice being lumped together like that in a way. It meant the whole experience wasn't something you were going through on your own, and reminded you there were lots of other little children in the same boat as you.

Then, one day, out of the blue, we were just told we were going home. Someone somewhere had decided it was safe to go home. I think I had been in my home in 'maybe Derbyshire' for about five or six months by then, so it was late summer, 1940. And I'd had no contact with my parents at all in that time. But much as I hadn't minded my time as an evacuee, I knew I wanted to be back with my mum and in London. I was clearly an East End kid through and through!

So it was back on the train down to London – by then I felt like an old hand at train travel – and then I remember we got on this old bus from the station to the church. And my mum was there waiting to pick me up. She was really pleased to see me and couldn't stop smiling and hugging me. 'I've missed you so much', 'I can't believe how much you've grown!', 'I'm proper happy to have you back', and all that kind of thing – looking back it must have been awful lonely and stressful for her, suddenly being without her two kids, and on her own at home most of the time. Scary too, I suppose, with constant talk of war, even if there had been very little proof of it. Anyway, it was great to be back, and London didn't seem to be that different – apart from the big elephants in the sky!

They were these things called barrage balloons, which were like huge grey balloons flying over London during the war. They were tied to these long cables that flew above the city over important buildings and the like. The idea, as I understand it, was that any low-flying bombers that came over the city couldn't go near them 'cause they'd get all tangled in the balloons or the wires.

But I remember the first time I saw one of them, which was almost as soon as I was back in London. There were a fair few near us, I suppose to protect all the factories and industry in the area, which would have played an important role during the war. Well, I was quite scared, they were like huge alien ships floating over us in the sky. But I soon got used to them – in fact, it was weird after the war when they disappeared.

The only time I ever see them now is if I go by a car showroom or something, and they have a barrage balloon floating above them advertising that the garage is there. Not quite the same effect, is it!

Tommy came home a week or so later than me, and

what I remember the most that had changed about him was he was in long trousers. Before he went he was always in shorts, short trousers like, but when he came back they were long. It was like he had gone all posh and grown up!

And fitting with the East End way of living in the present, me and him never talked about what we had done as evacuees, so I don't even know where he went to, or what he thought of his time away. We never even got around to talking about it as adults. I never asked them questions, it's one of those things. I guess we were both just pleased to be back in London, and got on with our lives there. As with everything else at that time you lived in the current moment and coped with that – the past was something you had lived through, rather than memories and stories to be gone over and over and discussed. It's a shame though really, looking back, 'cause I'd like to have known what he got up to and to have compared stories. Someone told me afterwards that it might have been Maidenhead he had gone to, as a lot of his schoolmates went there, but I have no idea. I just know it was a different place to me, and that was it.

Instead, by then we were focused on dealing with the reality of a London where the war wasn't actually over, but was just beginning.

THREE

The Bombing Begins

I don't know why we were brought back to London when we were – from what I can tell, the war had hardly even begun, let alone ended. But I don't suppose people realized that at the time. It's not like they were handed the official start and end dates to work around. Besides, East End families are rightly close knit, and a lot of parents probably felt they didn't want to be without their kids a moment longer and had them brought back. I suppose the lack of bombing and 'the phoney war' idea made everyone think that the war was over. Either that or maybe our parents just decided we were as safe in London with them as we were elsewhere in Britain with strangers. I've no idea, and it was never discussed, but either way, it was definitely a war that we were living through just weeks later.

I was still so young – coming up to five – so I don't

remember the actual night the bombing started. Looking back, I must have returned to London at the worst time – just as the Blitz was about to start. As far as I know, there was hardly any warning of the first attack, but from 7 September until 2 November 1940, London was bombed daily.

Oh, I remember those bombs through the Blitz, and there were plenty of them, fifty-seven long nights of 'em to be exact – and that was just for starters. But at least the British government had seen it coming, so by then there were systems set up to try and help you survive, and we soon got used to the routines.

Every time an air raid started you had to run out of the flats and down to the shelter. It was like this purpose-built shelter round the back of the flats in the gardens. These strange underground bunkers had sprung up while I was evacuated, the idea being that you would be hidden and unharmed when a bomb dropped. I think they did their job for most people.

What would happen was the sirens would start, and you would stop playing or whatever you were doing, and run through the gardens, then down these stairs and through a door into this kind of room made of brick-work and wooden frames. It was cold and horrible down there and smelt of damp and the paraffin from the oil lamps that were used to keep the place lit.

There would be loads of people crowded in – pretty much everyone reacted to the sirens – although there were a lot of shelters, so people went to different ones depending on where they were at the time. There were a few bunk beds down there that people would sit on, all huddled together, with kids on their parents' laps. And some of the elderly people brought chairs down to sit on, but other than that, there was only the floor. You could try and sleep, but there wasn't really the space, so instead people would sit in silence, or talk quietly.

You never knew how long you would be down there. Mostly it was about half an hour, but sometimes it would be through the night as well. If you were asleep and then the siren went off they were the worst air raids. I remember being literally dragged along and down the stairs by my mum sometimes when I was just too tired to move. She'd always talk in a whisper, as though she thought the Germans might hear us or something, but the urgency in her voice would be clear. 'Come on, Pat, get yourself up, we have to get to the shelter. NOW! Pick your feet up. Have you got your mask?' Then when you got there you would be pushed inside, all crushed like. It wasn't nice.

Sometimes it was total silence while you were down there, you couldn't hear anything at all, and that was good. But other times you could hear sounds from above but not clearly. Like muffled kinds of thuds, or just dull bangs. Then you got worried 'cause you knew when you came back out buildings were going to be missing, and there was always a chance it would be your home.

And, of course, although the idea was the shelters were safe, they weren't guaranteed to keep you alive. A direct hit to ours would probably still have meant bye bye Pat. So sounds of bombs close by put you on edge for that reason too.

You'd always get someone who'd be especially jumpy. 'What's that? Did anyone hear that thud? It's definitely near us. In fact, I think that was my home, it's over that way. The next one's going to be right here in this shelter. We should make a run for it!' And they'd get themselves worked up until some kind soul gave them reassurance, or a gruffer person told them to 'shut their mouth and hush, before you send the children into a panic'. When the threat was over, the sirens would sound again to tell you it was safe, that was it finished.

Sometimes, though, if the attack wasn't too bad, we didn't bother with the shelter. I remember one time the sirens started and me and Tommy were about to run down to the shelter, when my mum said, 'In here, quick!' and lifted up the kitchen table, which, if you remember, I said doubled as the lid of a bath. And the three of us clambered in there instead, all hunched down, and my mum pulled the lid down over us. Oh, that was uncomfortable and cramped. But it seemed more homely as well, me and Tommy lying on Mum, while she kept her arms around us. At least we weren't crowded in with other people, and hadn't had to make the mad dash to the shelter.

When the all-clear went and we climbed back out, stretching to get our muscles working again, my mum explained to us that she had known the raid wasn't going to be so bad. 'From now on, when I say, we can just go in the bath rather than the shelter.'

Well, we were happy enough with that, so from then on we spent some of the easier raids sheltered in our bath.

How we knew how bad the attack was going to be – if it was worthy of a shelter run, or just a bath dash – was thanks to the radio. Although I was still learning to interpret what they were saying, my mum knew instantly – it was like a real lifeline to know what was going on. They would be telling you, 'oh, these kinds of aircrafts have just bombed so and so, and are now flying inland towards so and so', and it got so she could work out what that meant for the East End. I forget now which ones, but certain bombs or planes meant we had to go to the shelter, and other ones meant we could just go in the bath.

All everyone did at this time was talk about the war, who was winning, the latest kind of bomb or plane that had been spotted, what they'd like to do to those Germans, the latest thing on rations, etc., and it was always on the radio. There was just non-stop chat about it and announcements, which didn't make any sense to me in the beginning. But Mum always made sure the radio was on, and over time I guess it soaked into me and I learned to translate some of what they were saying. Or at least I knew certain words or sentences, or the way that they were said that told me if it was good or bad news.

You never really saw the bombs actually falling – if all went to plan, you were well hidden away by the time they did. Then when the all-clear sounded, you would give it five or ten minutes just to be sure, and come up from the shelter and go back to your house – if you had one. People would come up from underground and look around and there was nothing there. Just a big, gaping hole where their home used to be. Oh, it was terrible. I don't know how people got through that really.

We'd come up out of the stairs into air full of dust and dirt, and rubble still flying around, and you'd know it was bad news for someone. You only hoped no one had died. But somehow you could always tell straight-away if someone had been killed. It sounds daft, but when people talk about the smell of death, it's true. You really could smell in the air if someone had died. It was an awful smell, like nothing I could describe. But you'd know one day if you smelt it what I was talking about, even with no one telling you.

So yes, you'd get out of the bunker, pull your mask up or put a scarf over your mouth to try and breath, and walk around to see what had happened.

Most people in our area weren't well off, so they were living in a council house or flat, and wouldn't have had any insurance on their home or items like you do today. So that was it. If their home had gone, their whole life had been blown to pieces, they had nowhere to go and nothing of their things left. You would hear screaming and crying from a particular road or area after you came up, as someone suddenly realized they were the one who had lost everything this time round.

But people were proper neighbours in them days. Everyone would help you look through the rubble when it was cooled down and safe, to see if anything could be saved. Although it wasn't always safe to go rooting through the remains. I remember my brother doing it once and it was a bad idea. He fell over a bit of shrapnel climbing around a bombed-out house, and cut his knee open. He had to take his shirt off and wrap it round his leg to try and stop the bleeding. At the time I thought it served him right 'cause I reckoned he wasn't so much being helpful as nosey!

You'd get the odd person scavenging too, trying to see if they could find anything to take from the rubble. Helping themselves to any belongings of the poor soul whose house had already been blown up. But then it was rare – I think if it was the case nowadays that people's houses in London were getting blown up, you'd get a lot of that. Back then it was much more about everyone looking out for another.

And everyone would go, 'come to my house, you got nowhere to go', and people would offer up some of their belongings, and let the poor homeless souls stay with them. It would never happen that they would just be left to deal with it alone. Everyone really pulled together.

Then again, maybe you could say they were the lucky people – they had lost things, but they were still alive. A lot of people got killed, mainly because they hadn't made it to the shelter in time. Never a close friend of mine, thank goodness, but people I vaguely knew in the area. I'd hear my mum discussing the names of victims with some auntie or another, and work out who had died that way. I'm not sure I really took it in, though. Their death just seemed like a fact, sort of removed from our family's life. Sometimes people would be running to the shelter when a bomb went off. Or they might even still be in their house looking for their things – people would bring their valuables to the shelter, as they were so worried about losing them. But sometimes the moments searching for those things when the warning went off is what killed them. You didn't always get much notice, so you never knew how long you had between the siren and a bomb maybe landing on you. Being as quick as you could was really the best way. I'd grab anything important that was right by me, but other than that I never spent time searching or going out of my way.

We really got it bad in London with all the bombing. It was all around. I don't know how we got through it. It shows what people actually can deal with, if they have no choice.

From time to time my dad would come home on a break, for a couple of weeks at a time. My mum would get all excited, and save the best food for those times, and make an effort with her appearance – something she didn't normally have the time to do. But to be honest, I hardly noticed him being there. He was a stranger to me at this point, so it hardly mattered to me whether or not I saw him. That might sound cold, but it's just a matter of fact. I didn't know him.

He'd always make an effort, though, and I remember

him being nice and joining in the odd game with me. He'd also have stories of the fighting and what they had done on the ship, but I never got to hear the tales – they were stories just for boys, so only Tommy got told them. Not that I minded – I wasn't very interested in them at that time anyway. Hearing about battles at sea miles away had no impact on my life – it was only the bombs over London that had any effect on me.

We got bombed a lot around where I lived – different places would get hit, but much as our block of flats were big, incredibly we never got bombed. The Germans never got them at all in any of their attacks, thank goodness. They did get houses near us, though. It was strange 'cause they were the smaller low houses, that you think they wouldn't have aimed for, but they were the ones that got blown right to the ground. Maybe they were aiming for us and missed, I will never know. I do know they always seemed to hit strange things – I'm not sure their aim was all that good from their planes all the way up in the sky!

Or maybe we were just good at sticking to the black-outs round my area. That's what they called it at night when the idea was that the whole area looked black from the sky, so that no German plane could spot where there were houses. One person with their lights on and curtains open could give it away, so they were very strict.

You'd have a black blind that you had to pull down

as soon as it was getting dark, and to be sure that you did, there was an air raid warden who would come round with a torch checking up on everybody. And if anyone had a light on that was showing, or their blind up, they would shine the torch through your window and shout 'turn that light off!' or 'pull that blind down!'

Most nights it meant you just went to bed early, 'cause with the lights out there wasn't a lot else to do other than maybe sit listening to the wireless in the dark to find out what was going on.

Although you could have candles, mind, or gas lighters on the wall on a very dim setting if the blind was pulled well down and sealed shut 'cause you couldn't even have a crack of light shining through.

They also missed a lot of buildings 'cause of the barrage balloons. From what I got told, those strange floating elephants did a good job at protecting London.

It's funny the things that never got hit, even without the help of a barrage balloon. Like some of the churches – all the houses roundabout them would get hit, but the churches would stay standing. They might sometimes lose their bell towers or what have you, but that was it. They always seemed untouchable or something.

But sadly my church, All Hallows, was hit. The main section of the church got blown up by a bomb in 1940. I don't remember the night it happened. I was too young when we went in the main bit to remember what it looked like, to be honest. It was shut for years – until 1955, I'm told, until there were the funds to repair it. Instead, services were held in a hall at the back of the church, that did us fine. They are all converted to flats now, mind you, from what I know now, and the bombed bit of the church has been rebuilt and reopened.

That Bilberry House and the flats around it didn't get hit was probably a particularly good thing for my nan – because it was impossible to get her in the shelter!

Oh, she was great, my nan. She was my dad's mum, and the kind of properly classic eccentric person you just don't get around today. She lived in a flat across the road from us, and she was deaf as a beetle. It was terrible. When the air raids used to start, my mum would panic and be like, 'Go down and tell Nanny quick, run around!' Me and my brother would run down the stairs and across the road, and there would be Nan standing looking out the window. She was always standing there, watching what was going on in the street below, and she would wave and shout at us 'Cooeeee!' and we'd be going, 'Nan, the bombs!' but she would just keep smiling and waving. 'Coooeeee!' In her own world she was.

The bombs would be dropping all around, and we used to try and coax her down as quickly as possible. Not her, though. We'd have to race up the stairs to get her, but by the time she got down the stairs and was on her way to the shelter, the siren would be going to say the air raid was finished!

Oh, I remember her, she was a great character. She was called Polly Spicer. Old Polly Spicer they used to call her. 'Here comes ol' Poll,' people would say, and she would come along and holler and hoot, you know, being deaf – I do take after her 'cause I do holler sometimes! But you could hear her for miles on.

She always wore black – which is probably where I get it from, as I'm pretty fond of that colour myself – and she had these two plaits that went round her ears like something out of *Heidi*. She would wear this black frock and she'd never wear a coat, but she would have this big blanket thing wrapped around her face. But the funniest thing was this kind of pinafore with a zip she wore all the time. It was like what they have on the stall holders, those apron things that tie at the back and hold their money. Well, she would keep all her money, policies, letters and documents in it. She put it on first thing of a morning, and took it off last thing at night before putting it under her pillow. She used to just carry it about with her because she thought if she died, or anything happened to her, she would have everything with her. It's not that she didn't trust people not to steal them – them days you didn't have robbers, you had your street door just lying open all the time. But it became her thing – she would trot along with everything she owned of value in her pinny. A proper unique old lady. I had a lot of time for my nan, and despite her eccentric ways, she was a real family person, and was always checking in with everyone that they were doing well.

It wasn't just the bombs that killed people at that time. Every now and then you would hear news of someone killed fighting in the war.

My dad had ten brothers and two sisters – a big family even in those days. But four of his brothers were killed taking part in the war, and they died young, ever so young.

Two of them were only sixteen when they died 'cause they had gone in the Army and Navy early. Obviously in them days you were told if you were a man that you had to go to war, but they went before they needed to. Before they were forced to sign up. I was told they had wanted to get away from London 'cause there was no work about and what have you. But they were gone away for a couple of months, and next thing you know they got killed. The amount of people that died, it was just awful, and while Nan wasn't the kind of person to let us see how upset she was, I can only imagine looking back how horrible it must have been for her losing her sons like this.

It was such a different way of living to today, it must seem completely strange to anyone not alive then, but that's just the way it was. It was such a terrible thing to live through the war, I don't think if it happened today half the kids could get through it. I really don't think they could suffer it. You had to have a different mentality and way of thinking to survive it that I don't think people today have. Then again, people are tougher than you know, so maybe that spirit would kick in if needed.

FOUR

Rags and Ration Books

The war wasn't all about death and bad things, though, there were some good times too. Especially after the Blitz ended in May 1941, when we weren't living with daily air raids and a constant fear of death and destruction. In the same way that people helped out those who had lost their homes, there were lots of other examples of people showing they had good hearts. And one of these meant going to church got a lot more fun, 'cause while the war was on, you got a present from a stranger after the service!

Up until then I went to All Hallows every Sunday with my mum. Then in the afternoon I'd go to Sunday school. Most people did back then – it's not like today when a churchgoer is a rare thing. Them days pretty much everyone put on their Sunday best and headed to church.

My dad, when he was around, didn't go unless he had to – he'd be having his pint instead – and I'd be like, 'Oh, I don't want to go', but anyhow I used to have to, and my mum would drag me over. I don't remember Tommy coming much either, maybe a couple of times, but I think he was off at Scouts and that – doing boys' things as boys do.

When the war was on, you would come out of the church afterwards, and there was this elderly lady and man – I say elderly because I was a kid then, and at that age you think everyone is old. They may have only been about thirty! But in my mind they were old. And they always had these two big sacks, one would be full of cards and one would be parcels. They would say to the kids as they came out the church doors, 'dip in, you can have one, come on, dip in'. And inside the sack would be parcels from abroad that people sent over because the war was on and they thought we might be in need, so it was like their way of helping us out.

So you would pick out a parcel from each sack, but you wouldn't open it, it would be like, 'I'll wait until I get home' so you could draw out the excitement of it. Then you'd get home and open it, and there might be a little T-shirt in it, or some knickers and a pair of stockings, or a blouse or skirt. Or other times it wasn't clothes but hair ribbons and clips, all different things like that.

And inside you would get an address on a card, saying, 'this is from', for instance, 'Mary in Australia' or so and so. They would come from all over the world. And you could write and thank them very much for what they had given you.

The present from the other sack would be a pack of cards, like Christmas cards or birthday cards, done up with a bow.

Sometimes, I admit – I feel bad to think it now – I would be ungrateful and think 'what do I want that for?', if I was unlucky and pulled out something I didn't want. But then you could trade it with someone else, for something you wanted instead. Most of the time, though, it was something really good – and always new, not second-hand, or dirty or anything. And I always remember them being done up prettily in paper. It was strange to think of someone in another bit of the world picking out a present to send someone they didn't know. A bit like those shoeboxes of toys or whatever that we send from the UK to poor countries these days, I suppose.

It was a great encouragement to go to church anyhow! As the war gradually finished, it faded out, but to me it has stayed as one of those memories of nice gestures the war brought out in people.

As well as being kind, one of the reasons those parcels were so important was 'cause most clothing and food were restricted at that time, so they really made a difference to what we could get in our shopping. What I mean is, there was rationing, so people were only allowed to get a certain amount of particular foods and clothes. You had an amount you were legally allowed to have.

It was something that came in slowly. Everyone always seems to think it came in as one big lifestyle change, that it was announced in one go, 'The war has started, everything is rationed!' But it was slow and in bits, almost so you didn't notice it happening like. Food was first, and then clothes.

Not that I really remember the first few bits being introduced – I was only four or five at the time, so just ate what I was given and didn't really notice any difference. I suppose there must have been rationing when I was in Derbyshire too, but we wouldn't have noticed it, 'cause being a farm they grew most of the food for themselves anyway or got it from one of their animals. In fact, I don't remember the woman there going shopping once at all.

The first things to start getting rationed were butter, sugar and bacon, and you knew how much you could have from your ration book. I can remember the ration book clearly. It was like this small notebook and there was one per person. The grown-ups' books were a kind of pale yellowy brown, while my brother and me had blue books. My mum used to guard all ours very closely – she'd keep them in her handbag. Back then, women always carried a handbag with them. It was a woman's privilege, which basically meant no one else was allowed to go in it. You respected it as her property. So not even my dad or me would have ever opened it, even just looking for house keys or anything. Mum would carry everything important inside her bag – money, keys, documents, a handkerchief and at that time, as I say, the ration books. Inside was a list of what you could have, what you were entitled to, so half a pound of cheese or the likes.

You would take the book to the shop when you went and the shopkeeper would stamp it to say you had got your portion, so you couldn't try and buy it again elsewhere. It was a way to keep the prices from going through the roof I suppose.

At one point it seemed like most things were on ration – I remember bacon, eggs, cheese, milk, sugar, butter, rice, cereals, jam and biscuits all being in the ration books. Even some fruit and veg were on ration at one time, and sweets – which is where my mum's job in the sweet factory came in so useful!

All the rationing made sure you definitely didn't waste anything. Not like today, when you can buy half a dozen eggs, a loaf of bread and bacon, and think nothing of putting it in the bin if you haven't got around to eating it before it goes off a week later. Them days you wouldn't have dared waste anything. You cooked everything and you had to eat it. None of this 'Oh, the bacon's gone dry, the eggs have gone off' kind of thing. It's a shame when I see today how much goes to waste really.

The ration books didn't make things perfect, though. As with everything, there were some people who managed to find different ways to get more than their share. From what I know there was a pretty healthy black market going on the whole way through the war, so that poor people who didn't have a lot of money would sell on their rations at a higher price to try and earn some money. It would just happen quite openly in the street. Like you'd be walking along and you'd get someone come near and say quietly 'Wanna buy eggs?' or 'You need sugar?' or so on. I imagine some of the shopkeepers were at it too, or found ways around stamping things, or saving better cuts of meat and that for people who paid more. I've heard people talk about it since, but it wasn't something I knew was happening when I went to the shops with my mum. As far as I know she never bought any food like this, tempting though I suppose it must have been at times. She just kept the food really basic and straightforward, not that I realized it at the time, as it was all I knew. Big roast dinners and cakes were to be a thing of the future!

Rationing carried on for a few years after the war, but it slowly faded out over time. I think I was about eighteen before it was all completely scrapped – meat was the very last thing that was still on the list. Then you could finally go in a shop and buy what you wanted, which was strange for me, as I had lived so much of my childhood having to be careful. Not that I was so rich I could go wild mind, just that you didn't have to consider if you had had your share of something for that week or not when you were working out what to have for dinner.

The way it was then – where your main worry was getting enough of everything to eat – also meant I didn't really understand the idea of people going on a diet when I first came across it. You never heard anyone saying 'Oh, I've got to lose weight' or 'You need to drop a few pounds'. It might sound funny, but it was seen that you were lucky to get food, so why would you start depriving yourself of it? It just wasn't something that you'd consider. And people were much more factual about weight. If they got bigger, they got fat. If they got smaller, they got skinny. That's just how it was – you didn't worry about it, and you also didn't avoid saying it to save someone's feelings or whatever. It probably meant people had a much healthier attitude to weight. It wasn't something people got hung up about.

Not that there weren't issues of course. A friend I knew around my way, when I look back, was quite clearly suffering from anorexia. She was painfully thin, and got to looking more like a small child than a teenager. But I never even knew what anorexia was, and I don't suppose most people did, so we always thought she was just very skinny. It's only now with hindsight that I can see that's pretty much definitely what was wrong with her. Not that I could say what caused it, and she always seemed a happy enough little thing, despite her weight.

But anyhow, as well as food, as I say, clothing was rationed as the war continued. I think there wasn't the material arriving in the country any more for lots of clothes to be made. Or maybe there wasn't the manpower to make them. Each person was given a book filled with coupons that you could swap for clothes. You had to pay money too, but the coupons allowed you to buy them in the first place.

These were little pink books which had different colour coupons you could use depending on what time of year it was. Different types of clothes were worth different amounts, so you had to work out what you needed the most. So say you had sixty coupons in total for the year, a coat might 'cost' ten or fifteen of them plus the actual money you were paying, so you had to really need that coat to use up so many coupons. And you can imagine what it was like if someone wanted to get married in those days. Well! From what I heard sometimes the shopkeepers would turn a blind eye for a bride-to-be, to try and help them get their dress, but mostly they just had to use old dresses, or make do with a nice frock they already owned.

Generally, instead of buying new items, the attitude was much more to mend clothes. It was like this before the war from what my mum said, just because people didn't have the money to be buying new clothes all the time, but the war made it even more set in people's minds. New clothes were a luxury, so could only be bought when actually necessary. There was a saying the government would repeat to everyone on the radio and in leaflets to try and encourage us during the war, and that was 'make-do and mend'. Though as I say, that way of thinking already existed in the mind of working-class folks. You just didn't have the clothing like you've got today. You never went out and bought a new dress or top to go out like I see my grandchildren doing. They won't wear some items more than a few times, whereas we had an outfit and wore it from one year to the next. We'd have been over the moon to even have a few of the things they have now.

No, you didn't have the money to buy everything – you were, in other words, hard up. I think as a kid I only had my school uniform, and then, say, a couple of dresses besides that. And we looked after them – well, you had to, because you couldn't buy nothing else, and if you got a little tear in it you'd sew it up. My clothes were generally little cotton dresses. Girls then wouldn't have worn trousers or jeans. Oh, and a hat. I had this little silly beret that I always used to wear. Not that I thought it was silly – I loved it! Girls back then always had little woollen hats or berets that they wore when they left the house, it was just the done thing. Any old pictures from back then, and we are all sure to be there in our silly hats!

But the only time I really got something new was maybe very occasionally for a wedding or at Christmas. Then my mum would take me shopping as though it was a big treat, or later, one of my aunts would take me. We'd go over to a department store in Stratford called Boardmans that was like another world. It was huge, and there was a different floor for everything. One for furniture, one for women's clothes, one for men's . . . I know that is quite normal these days, but then, when everything was done in small local shops, department stores were rare, and going there meant a big day out! People would come from all around to visit Boardmans.

One thing I remember is that they didn't have tills – they were a step above that. Most other shops had the old cash registers, or the very small shops did the payments by hand, working out the maths on a piece of paper. But not Boardmans, no, what they had was this kind of payment system where the money shot off to a clerk at the back of the store.

It's not easy to explain, 'cause if you have never seen it, it's hard to imagine. But how it would work is the shop assistant would take what you wanted to buy, add up what you owed, and take the money off you. Then it would be put inside this pot with a lid on it that would be shut down, then it would go in a tube on the wall, and whizz along to the clerk who was sat in an office somewhere else in the building. He would be sat there in his office, and would do the maths to check it was all correct, and put your change back in the pot with a receipt, and send it back to the shop assistant to give back to you. I've no idea what made the tubes move – gusts of air, I suppose – but it was pretty fascinating to watch as a kid. I guess it was the ultimate in technology then!

It was a much more drawn-out process to pay than it is today, but then you weren't in a rush to get in and out of the shop in the same way. So it wasn't like people were huffing and puffing behind you in a long queue or anything. It was part of the big experience of a day out at Boardmans!

That way of paying existed a long time ago as I only really remember it as a little girl, so I guess it must have changed to more modern tills pretty soon after. Visiting those stores was a real treat – but there was no way it could distract from the old make-do and mend way of life!

There used to be an old rag-and-bone man who would come round Devons Road, but he never got much trade near ours at that time. No one had much that they were willing to give up. He was after old clothing or bits of rag, and would give you a couple of bob in return, but we were too busy making those old clothes and rags work for us again.

But he'd still keep trying, pulling up each week in his old horse and cart, shouting out 'money for yer ol' rags' and all that, but yeah, we rarely had anything for the poor fella. Shame we don't have those rag-and-bone men any more – I suppose giving clothes to the local charity shop is the closest equivalent.

I remember too what you had to do with stockings to keep them being used as long as possible. You wore stockings and suspender belts in them days – to my knowledge I don't think tights were even invented, or if they were, we didn't know about them. Anyway, you would stitch up your stockings if they got a tear or a hole, and if you lost the button on your suspender belt, you put a little sixpence coin in instead to hold them up. The things we used to do! Mind you, it worked just as well.

It might sound silly but even now I still look after my clothes. Like, I'll still buy new things, but I'll fix them when something goes wrong. If I've lost a button I'll find a new one and sew it on, or if I've caught a top and got a little hole in it, then I'll mend it. I think it's too inbuilt in people of my generation for that to ever change – and I don't think it's a bad way to be, neither.

FIVE

A Heart of Gold

By then I had started at school. I went to Devons Road School, a girls' primary school in Knapp Road, just a couple of streets away from Bilberry House. I think I started in September 1941, when I was five, nearly six. It's still there, although now it's called the Clara Grant Primary School, after the headmistress who was there up until 1927 – so before I was even born.

Although it might sound weird, school was never very important to me. It was something I had to do, just 'cause everyone else did it, but it wasn't something that played a big part in my life, or that I enjoyed very much. When I think back to being a kid, it's not something that appears in many of my memories.

Don't take me wrong, I didn't get a hard time off other kids or anything, it just wasn't really for me. So I don't remember that much about it – it seemed irrelevant.

I don't know if what I got was a good education, but I brought all my kids up well, so I think it must have been enough.

What I mostly remember is leaving the house late for school as I wasn't that keen to go, and running down the road to get there – it was only about a ten-minute walk, but I think I ran it in five most days! I'd walk – or run – to school with Winnie, who was in the same class as me. Then when we got to the school, we'd go through an archway to get into it. It said 'Girls and Infants' overhead, 'cause the boys went to a separate school down the road called Knapp Road School, which is where Tommy went.

Anyway, when I got there each morning, I'd take my coat off and get on with lessons. I think the classroom was covered in white tiling or brickwork. I remember it being quite sterile, but it's really not clear in my mind, it was so long ago. There might be memories from my infant school and my senior school later on that I am mixing together.

In the very young years, the best bit of the day was after lunch when you got given a little bottle of milk, then you got to go and lie down and have a sleep. All the kids did it. I think it was called rest time. When we were very little I think there were actual camp beds to sleep on, but when I was older, I remember just having to lie with my head on my arms on the desk.

If you were skinny you got different treatment, though. Children who were very thin went to a different bit for their sleep. Kind of like this tent classroom outside. Then they were given a bottle of malt, as well as the milk. I think the idea was that these kids needed feeding up and being made healthy. I suppose looking back some of them were actually quite badly underfed and malnourished, and the fresh air and malt was to help build them up. It might sound strange in today's world where the opposite is more the problem now, but then, well, that's how it was.

As we got older we did most of the usual academic subjects, history, sums, and the likes, but I didn't really enjoy any of them. I think most of my learning has come from life. So like I'm quite cute in money business! But that came from just doing the shopping, budgeting for a family, my later jobs . . . not from school. And for the kind of life I knew I would end up leading, things like history and geography seemed pointless. I wasn't even a lover of reading. Working through some novel didn't interest me in the slightest. What I needed to learn about was how to get on with the day-to-day life that I would probably end up leading – how to get a basic job, run a household, be a good housewife, bring up kids . . . but of course that wasn't what they were teaching, not in my school anyhow.

I did enjoy the more artistic side of school, though. I didn't mind art and dancing and P.E., which then was much more focused on keeping fit than team sports. So like we didn't do hockey or netball or any of those things. It was more seeing how many times you could climb up and down this big ol' rope that hung from the gym ceiling. Or skipping with a rope, or table tennis.

I was probably a pretty average student in the eyes of the teachers. Although, weirdly, I can't really remember any of them, so I don't suppose they can have made an impression on me. School was something annoying that had to be got through, so I did it with the minimum effort and fuss needed to get by unnoticed.

There was the cane then, of course. I don't think I got it – in fact I can't have because I am sure I'd remember it. I think, generally, girls didn't get caned much. It was seen as a thing to keep naughty boys under control more than girls.

The first time someone was naughty they would cane them in front of the class. They'd be called up and have to hold their hands out. You'd kind of wince for them as it hit their hands – it made such a 'thwack!' noise. Then if someone was really and truly naughty, or played up all the time, they'd get sent down to the headmistress's office and they'd get a real going over. I remember people coming back from there with their hands and the back of their legs really torn to strips. It wasn't nice – but then I guess you only had to behave and you'd avoid it.

It's not just the punishment that has changed in schools, but also the racial mix of them. All the kids in my school were white. Although East London is a proper mix of all races and nationalities now, then it was very much filled with a white population, people who had lived there all their lives, whose parents had lived there, and their parents, and so on, and mostly every generation having even lived in the same house.

I can't remember how old I was the first time I saw someone with black skin, but it was a shock, I do remember, 'cause it's not what you were used to, so it looked strange to me. Also – and I can't believe I am saying this as it is so awful – but we were warned by the adults to 'keep away from the coloureds, in case they slit your throat'. The poor fellas were obviously harmless as could be, looking back, but at the time we had that idea put in our head, and we'd run and hide if we ever saw a black person coming.

I did see a few Chinese people from time to time 'cause there was a kind of area known as China Town building up around Millwall, but again, it'd be like, 'There's a Chinaman coming, hide!' Oh, it's terrible, isn't it? It was just fear of the unknown, I suppose, and really, just ignorance from older people being passed on.

Anyway, the old headmistress of my school, Clara Grant, who I mentioned at the start of the chapter, was something of a local hero. In fact, my weekly highlight far and away was a trip to see Clara Grant.

She was long retired by then, and oh, she was a grand old lady was Clara Grant. She was a local resident, and was one of the loveliest ladies going. She lived down Fern Street, which was the next road along from All Hallows church, across Devons Road from Watts Grove. Down there were rows and rows of terraced houses. All the roads near there looked the same. These tiny dark-coloured brick houses were identical, but somehow had their own character too.

And I swear Clara Grant was happy to help every child in the world. What would happen was every Saturday morning, children would be queued up outside her house for miles and miles. I'm not joking, the street was filled with kids patiently lined up, waiting to go in and see her.

When you got to the front of the queue you had to go under an arch to get into her house. The arch was about four foot high and above it was 'Enter Now Ye Children Small, None Can Come Who Are Too Tall'. And you had to prove that you were small enough to get under the arch. It was Clara Grant's way of making sure only people young enough got to see her. And I'll tell you what, while most kids were desperately hoping to keep growing taller in the rest of the world, round our way, everyone was trying to reverse the process! You've never seen such a stooping bunch of children as those waiting in line to see Clara, and clearly reaching borderline height. People would be doing all sorts as they got near the front – taking off their shoes to keep them as small as possible, or practising pulling their head down into their neck somehow!

But if you made it through the arch – and you could be sure that one of Clara's group of volunteer helpers would be watching closely – then you would get into her house, which was this really old house, and I remember it always smelled of lavender and musk. It was like a proper old person's house the way it was decorated – or actually it was three houses joined together if I remember rightly. She would be in there, this very small, very elderly lady, and you would hand over a farthing and in exchange you got a parcel, or farthing bundle, as they got called. And it would be full of any kind of surprise – clothes, toys, handkerchiefs, marbles, whistles, shells, cards, pencils, bits of material . . . basically anything she thought would keep a child entertained. You didn't open them, but you brought them home and then in the secrecy of your own room saw what was inside. It was like you were getting Christmas or a birthday every week from Clara Grant, who ended up with the nickname the Bundle Woman of Bow.

She made a point of knowing as many of the local kids and their parents as possible, and if she knew that you were particularly hard up and she thought your family had no money for coal or things like that, she'd go, 'Here lovey' and dip her hand into her pocket for her purse, for she always had her purse on her. Then she'd give you 2 shillings and 6 pence or 5 shillings or something. It wasn't a lot – maybe 25p in today's money – but it always helped. Or she might give you a glass of lemonade or a biscuit if she thought you looked a bit on the scrawny side. Just whatever she thought you needed to help you out.

I haven't the foggiest why she did it all. I guess she just had a heart of gold and must've had a lot of money from somewhere. I think the farthing you paid for your parcel was more a gesture than something she needed, anyhow. Like something to make you feel you were buying your bundle, rather than being given it as charity. And she had all these women who had volunteered to help her. Looking back it was such a good thing. It had a really good feel about it all.

She was a strong woman too and seemed to make

things happen. Like, until her time we never had a bus that came down Devons Road. But she was the first person to get it to do that. The number 86 I think it was. I know that might not sound like much now, but it was a big deal then. We'd felt a bit left out of the loop with the buses, and it made life a lot easier for people when they didn't have a long walk to catch one.

I swear those Saturday mornings at Clara Grant's place are some of the best memories from my childhood. And actually, I think if you ask just about anyone who grew up around Bow at that time, they would tell you the same. It's a shame it doesn't run any more.

I suppose that's why people want to still remember her even now – she was someone for the East End to be proud of. So as I said at the start of this chapter, my old school, Devons Road School, has changed its name since to the Clara Grant Primary School, which seems very fitting.

Very suddenly, the bombing, which had pretty much been absent for three years, apart from the odd raid, started again properly in June 1944. It was quite a shock – although the shelters had remained in place, and we all still had our gas masks, we'd got quite out of the way of using them.

So things went back to how they had been in 1940,

except this time I was having to go down into the shelter at school rather than at Bilberry House when the sirens went off in the day. Whenever the siren started we all had to file down into these bunkers right under the school grounds. We'd have our gas masks with us, and the first couple of times it was fun – more like an underground adventure with your friends. But then it got boring, just sitting down in the cold and damp, waiting for the all-clear.

The teachers would try and keep everyone's spirits up by getting us to sing. I suppose it was a way to try and cover up any noises from outside that could scare us as well.

Other times, if there wasn't enough warning to get people to the shelters, I remember us all having to pull our masks on when the siren went off, and sometimes we just crawled under our desks. Imagine. What use would that be in saving us if a bomb had landed on the school?!

And something else had changed – the Germans were using different bombs this time, what we knew as a dreaded doodlebug. Oh, they were horrid. Everyone would say, 'A doodlebug is coming! Quick, get under!' And you'd hear this whistling sound that it made as it came closer in the sky, 'cause the doodlebug was this kind of flying bomb. And you wanted the whistle sound to keep going until it was well past you, 'cause when the whistle stopped, well, that was the bomb dropping. So, if it was over you . . .

I saw a film a while ago with doodlebugs in it, and the sound brought it back to me. I can't say as I liked it one bit.

But luckily the school itself never did get hit, though we had a very close call one day. The sirens had started and we had gone underground, and were probably singing songs as usual, when we felt the thuds. This time they felt closer and I think we all fell silent for a moment. When the siren for the all-clear sounded, and we climbed out into the open air, we could see that five houses facing the school on Knapp Road had completely vanished.

They were all knocked clean down to the ground. And muck and bits of brick were still flying around everywhere. There was smoke and dust just hanging in the air, and you could hardly see or breathe, but it was very quiet, really deathly quiet. Like everyone was in shock, and all the dust sucked every sound out of the air. And there was that death smell again. I remember it, it was horrible.

The teachers told us all to go home. We had to get ready quick and run along the road to our homes. I don't know if they were going over to help and needed us out of the way, or if they thought the bombs might come back over, but I remember getting my stuff and running the five minutes back to our flat. I was really scared and I was thinking how close it was to the school that the bomb had hit, and wondering what had happened to the people who lived in those houses.

At one point, the boys' school down the road from ours got hit by a bomb. It was turned almost instantly into a shell of a building. Luckily, though, it got bombed overnight, so, as far as I know, there was no one in it.

The next day the boys were walking up to their school to find it wasn't there – not that I'm sure a lot of them minded! But they didn't get to avoid school for long. They had to come and join our school, so we were all crammed into our building together – the number of pupils doubled in a day. They sorted out a new school building for them soon enough, though.

I've also been told since that one of the rooms in our school was used as a mortuary in the war. So that when anyone was killed locally, their body was brought to our school and laid out in there. I didn't know that at the time, thank goodness, as that would have been awful. I guess the kids would have been kept well away, and wouldn't have seen anything of what was going on.

Then in March 1945, the bombing eased up again

and things started to return to normal. There was talk that we were close to winning the war, but I didn't pay much attention. By this point in my life, Britain being at war was mostly all I knew.

SIX

The War is Over!

The war ended on 2 September 1945. I don't remember how I found out, though I imagine it was on the radio. I'm not sure anyone knew whether to believe it! The bombing had stopped a few months before, so we had known things were on the up, but it was still hard to take in. I didn't really know life without the war.

I remember a kind of unplanned gathering breaking out in the courtyard in front of our building and everyone just chatting and smiling and exchanging news and opinions. But the real celebrations were saved until the soldiers got home.

I don't remember the exact moment my dad got back. As I said before, I didn't really feel like I knew him, so to be honest, it would have been a much bigger moment for my mum. No doubt she was really excited to have him back.

And that day I suppose was the moment everyone really felt they could believe the war was definitely over and we were back to peace. Husbands, sons, fathers, they were all back with their families – at least those that had survived – and that's when the real party happened. Out in the courtyard and spilling out into the streets roundabout, everyone was gathering and spending the day dancing and singing along to gramophones that people had set up, and mostly giggling a lot. It was one of those days when everyone gets a bit giddy and excited about the future – although looking back, I'm sure there were those who couldn't be cheered up, who wondered at the price their loved ones had paid to get peace back.

But it wasn't like life changed for people overnight. Rationing still continued, damaged buildings still took months or years to be fixed, etc. But it was true – there was no more hiding in shelters. I don't really know what happened to them. I guess most of them got filled in. I think our one at Bilberry House did. As far as I can remember, it just got covered over and taken up as part of the gardens.

As for us, with Dad out of the Navy and living back with us properly, we settled into a bit of a new routine with him around. We were a proper family of four then, rather than a family of three.

It was good to have him around at that time, and to get to know him really – it is probably those next couple of years in my childhood when we had the best relationship. And I know most girls say this about their dads, but my dad really was handsome and so well turned out. He always had a lovely clean shirt on, and he was a collar and tie man – he would never sit down to eat or go anywhere without a collar and tie, no matter where he went.

And first thing of a morning he would shave – even if he didn't need to, he'd always do it. I remember him standing in his vest over the bathroom sink, with his brush and shaving stick, getting it all foamed up and running this razor all round his face and neck with proper concentration. He was good at it too – there was barely ever a fleck of blood or a nick on his face.

He started working as a painter and decorator, and did up all the big hotels in London. I can't remember most of them, as the names meant nothing to me then, but the one he used to talk about most was the Savoy. He loved doing jobs there, and would have done up most of the rooms in there at some point.

Whenever they had people who were 'specially famous or rich staying in the hotel, they could say if they wanted something done to the room. So if a celebrity was staying for a few days while they did radio shows or concerts or something, they might decide they didn't want the room that colour, or they'd want a bit of edging around something. Or that's what he used to tell me, anyhow.

And he became pretty popular with some of the big stars who used to stay there. Tony Bennett would always arrive and say, 'Can I have my painter and decorator back?' and he'd get him to do just what he wanted with the room. He was always nice and friendly to my dad, and used to say to him, 'How's your daughter getting on?' and all that. Dad loved it. He'd come home and be all like 'my pal Tony Bennett' and make out that they were like best friends or something.

Then there were a few famous women singers who he used to get on well with. I forget their names, although a few years later when Shirley Bassey was making a name for herself on the scene, I remember him mentioning her a few times. I can't remember the name of the earlier women, although they were hugely popular at the time. He was forever telling me stories about them, and I loved it – it was a world so different from mine.

He used to talk to them about me too, and one day one of them gave him one of her wigs to bring home to me to keep, as a present. I wasn't very old but I can always remember him walking through the door with this thing – it was great! And I used to play all sorts of games with it, trying it on and acting out like I was a famous singer myself. It was all curly, and if you brushed it, it would come up all big and bushy. It was a really lovely wig now I think about it. Probably worth a fair few bob, even without the celebrity connection, but I didn't notice that at the time. Instead me and one of my cousins decided to dye it. I remember her saying, 'Let's give it another colour'. Course in them days you didn't have proper hair dye, so we used ink. We had a little bottle of ink and a little thin paintbrush and we were putting colours in it like that. It was great fun and we added in lots of streaks of different colours over time. We ruined it in the end and then it got discarded. How awful is that? But it did provide hours of entertainment at the time – thanks to the lovely singer lady, whoever you were!

Sometimes my dad did well out of it too. I remember the number of times he used to bring home wallpaper and say, 'I did so and so's room, and only used three quarters of the paper', so he'd have like spare rolls. Or a tin of paint when the person changed their mind about the colour. Then he'd say, 'Oh, there might be enough here to do up that little room', so he was always redecorating our house. It was already paid for, so it wasn't like he was doing anything wrong, it was an added bonus of the job – I can always remember him saying that.

And unlike when he was off for weeks at a time in the Navy, when he was working a day job with normal hours, he would come back home every night. Everyone was happy and getting on, and everything just seemed quite light-hearted and relaxed. It was a good time.

My parents seemed really happy in their marriage. I never saw them hugging and holding hands and that, but I don't think people would do that in front of their children back then. But they just seemed to have an understanding of each other, and a similar humour. They worked well together, if you know what I mean. And I don't remember them ever having arguments, like some children say, 'My mum and dad are always fighting and rowing'. But I can't remember that at all. They just seemed very happy with each other.

My dad was close to his mum – my nan Poll. He'd go round there to visit and decorate her flat, and check if she needed anything, and she'd pop round to check on us as well. Me and Tommy would go round and visit her too, sometimes for Sunday lunch. But not as often as you might think, as she had so many children, there were a lot of people for her to divide her time between, and from what I could tell she was 'specially close to her two daughters, Maggie and Mary.

One thing I'll always remember about my dad around this time that used to make my mum roll her eyes but left me and Tommy in stitches, was his sayings. The things he used to come out with all the time! These proper classic old East End sayings that meant nothing at all really, but were just things he'd say. Like if you mentioned someone, and asked did he know them, he'd reply with, 'I used to chew bread for his mother's duck'. It makes no sense at all, but it was just a thing! It's typical of the East End to talk in riddles, there are loads of sayings here like that, and it's just part of what makes up the uniqueness of the area. It's one way to see if someone is local too, by seeing how they respond to a saying like that. I picked that duck saying up off my dad, and have left many of my grandkids looking at me all confused when I say it to them.

I got another similar one off an aunt.

'Do you know so and so?'

'Oh yeah, I used to scrub her doorstep.'

Again, who knows where it comes from, but it's something people said and I've picked up the habit. I still use both those sayings even today. The East End is still alive and well in me, and I suppose it's a bit of my dad in me as well!

The other good thing that happened once he was around every evening was we always sat down together to eat as a family. Looking back I'm glad we did that, but it was frustrating sometimes for a starving kid having to wait for Dad to get home and be seated before you could eat. We'd always be like 'Hurry up Dad!'

Every evening we had a hot meal. Meat and veg and all that business – pretty traditional stuff. Except for Fridays – Friday was always fish day. People quite often have takeaway on a Friday now, but it's a bit of anything isn't it, pizza or Chinese or the likes, but then it was always fish and chips. Mum would go out and buy her fresh fish in the day on a Friday, and then either boil it or fry it. My dad always especially liked fish Fridays 'cause his side of the family were fish people – he came from a family who'd run fish shops in the area for years.

As for breakfast in our house, it was always porridge or toast. There was nothing fancy mixed in with the porridge, mind, like today, no blueberries or honey or whatever, it was just plain or with sugar. The only difference you got was sometimes it was thick and sometimes soft, I guess depending on how much milk we had that we could use at the time, according to if it was still on ration. Then when it was the weekend, for a little extra treat you'd get a second slice of toast, or maybe a boiled egg with your breakfast.

We'd have lunch at school. You got it for nothing in them days, which was good, no bringing money to the canteen or what have you. Not that the food was great. I remember we had a lot of stews, or spam with potatoes and vegetables. I remember the desserts better – bowls of apple pie and custard, and helpings of semolina pudding. Warm filling food, I suppose, is what the catering staff were mainly aiming for.

You got no choice over the food you were given, though. Today people are all like 'I can't eat this because I am allergic to it' or 'I don't like that'. Them days you ate it and that was that. You didn't hear of vegetarians neither. You ate what you were offered by the school staff or you went without – it was tough luck.

But my favourite food of the week, my absolute treat, was a little bag of cockles and winkles and shrimps. One of my aunties was called Rosie Spicer, and I'm pretty sure I was actually related to her in some way on my dad's side of the family. And before you say anything about her surname, well, that wasn't necessarily a give-away 'cause there were a lot of Spicers in the area. I'm sure at one point if you did a big family tree, we were all related, but you didn't know the link with half of them. So yeah, Rosie was an auntie, but not like my dad's sister or anything.

Anyway, Rosie used to walk about Devons Road with this great big barrow, or barra', as we'd say, selling seafood. She had white bowls on the barra' filled with the winkles and cockles and all that kind of food, and she would sell them by the pint to anyone who came over to her. So if someone came and asked for a pint of winkles, she had this kind of metal jug, like a beer jug for a pint, and she'd dip it in the bowl, wipe her hand over the top to get it filled perfectly level with the rim, then pour them into a brown paper bag and charge however much it was for that.

I used to tag along with her on a weekend. Early every Sunday morning, her husband would load up the barra' for her, and she'd set off on her route, and I'd find her somewhere on the way.

'Winkles and shrimps!' she'd yell at the top of her voice as we walked along, and people would come out, all pleased to see her. And to keep me happy, she'd give me a little mixed bag of them for free. I used to love 'em.

She was a proper big character was Rosie. Everyone knew her and her barra', and came out to see her. She was right striking-looking too. A tall lady with long bright ginger hair, that she used to tie in two plaits at the side of her head and twirl into buns around her ears. The same as what my nan did. This was probably the closest there was to a hair fashion amongst older people, but like most things it was more to be practical than attractive. She was all about being practical was Rosie. You'd never see her in make-up or the likes, she was too busy working and getting on with her life. But she was sociable and liked a chat, and was probably one of the best known characters in the area. I don't suppose you get barra' ladies like that these days, although there are still huts outside some pubs in the East End selling shellfish like that, or on market stalls. My Auntie Rosie was well known for selling them in our area at the time, though.

In fact the whole of my dad's family was known for fish. They were in the fish trade, and were very good at it as far as I can tell. It's probably why I love my fish and shellfish so much – it's in my blood!

Rosie and some of my other aunts and uncles used to own an actual fish shop along Bow Common Lane – not very originally called Spicers' Fish Shop. But it was a great place, full of all sorts of fish and seafood. You'd be amazed at the amount of people who still say to me they remember that shop from their childhood, and so and so Spicer who used to sell them their fish. Folks especially remember the smells that used to come out of the shop.

I think the main smell that made an impression on people was the smoked fish. There used to be this smoke room in the shop, where my aunts and uncles would smoke fish in a traditional way that I don't think many places do any more. All my family did things like that in the proper way. They'd burn wood shavings, I think it was, and hang the fish on a long bit of rail above it. Then as the wood smouldered away underneath, the smoke soaked into the fish, which is partly good to preserve it and also 'cause it picks up the flavours. Different types of wood would create a different smell, and therefore a different flavour.

Mostly it was smoked haddock, kippers and mackerel that were done in this way. It doesn't sound like much describing it here, I don't suppose, but when it was done properly, oh, it had a great smell and taste. If you've never experienced it, get yourself to an old traditional shop and try it for yourself.

You could smell it the whole way down the street. It was like temptation calling you in! We'd get our fish from them cheaper, sometimes free, and sometimes paid for. Family discount I guess you'd call it.

I remember a daft trick a few of my fish family used to do to me, especially one of my uncles. You know on the top of a winkle there is like this little black bit that you pick off? Well, he'd be there with a winkle in his hand, and the next thing you knew he'd lean in and wipe your face, all friendly, like he was doing you a favour.

'What you got there on your face?' he'd say, looking all concerned.

Really he was sticking the black bit of the winkle on my face, so as I looked like I had a beauty spot. And sometimes you'd not realize what he'd done for ages after, 'til someone pointed it out. I fell for that one every time.

Around that time there was an actress called Margaret Lockwood who had made a beauty spot what I suppose you'd call her trademark, so it was seen as no bad thing to have one, and we all wanted to copy it. But putting a piece of seafood on my face wasn't the way forward . . . Instead, me and Winnie tried it ourselves with pen and ink. I'm not sure we ever quite pulled off the same kind of allure, though!

SEVEN

An East End Childhood

As far as what I did when I wasn't at school, well, it's hard to know how we passed the time. There really was not a lot to do – no television or anything like that, of course, and parents definitely didn't feel it was part of their job to entertain kids then. We were mostly left to our own devices, or if they did ask us to do something to pass the time, it mostly had a useful side attached.

One of my earliest memories of spending time with my mum was sitting doing knitting or crocheting or embroidering. She loved to embroider, and would always be doing different pillowcases or plain white tablecloths, just putting patterns on them to make them more interesting.

'Come over here and I'll show you what to do, girl,' she'd say.

I used to sit there and do it with her, while we listened

to the radio, or sat in concentrated silence. And as I got better she'd tell me, 'You've done a good job there girl, keep it up.' And I'd feel all pleased – I suppose I was actually a help in the end. It's a skill that a lot of people don't have but I made sure to pass it on to my lot, so I have shown my daughters and my granddaughters.

Knitting was, I suppose, more practical, but not as enjoyable. We'd knit clothes and things to wear. But wool was scarce at times, and you would never throw anything away, so you would have to pick apart one item to make the next. So say you had a jumper that you had got too big for, you had to sit and unpick all the rows of stitches and then use that same wool to knit yourself something else. It was quite a long task. I remember my mum saying, 'Right, sit there and undo that, and we'll see what else we can make out of it.' Then you did the knitting with these great big fat knitting needles, and this great big thick wool. She'd tell me bits of gossip from time to time while we were sat there, nothing too scandalous mind, or just talk through what she was going to make for dinner that day or what jobs she still had to do. Most of the time I was just listening, as though she were getting her thoughts in order out loud, but it made me feel grown up to hear it nevertheless.

I remember making these rugs called rag rugs out of old material – everyone made them and had them in their houses. You would cut strips of material, about an inch wide, from any old clothes that were beyond repair. All different patterns and colours. Then you would have a sack that was like your base, and you would make a hole in it for the material to go through. Then with this hook you would pull through a loop of the material. And you done it up in a knot, and kept doing that over and over, until the whole sack was covered, and then you had a new mat – or carpet, if it was big enough. It was very time-consuming and could take months and months to do. But it was a creative way to recycle! And of course it kept you busy.

There was just this attitude that play time for kids wasn't that important, not like the way it is seen today. Every free minute was expected to be used for something productive where possible. I guess necessity dictated that. So often if I went round an auntie or uncle's house, they'd see me as an extra pair of hands for a job.

I never forget one of my real aunts, Maggie, one of my dad's two sisters, who had a couple of boys. I'd arrive and she'd be on me instantly.

'You bored, girl? Wait a minute, there is a bag of socks here. Come on, grab that needle and cotton, sew that up, do this, do that . . .'

You would sew over the sock, and back again, and back again, like that, darning it 'til there was no hole and they could wear it again. It was part of looking after your gear.

Oh, and I remember a popular trick of one particular aunt. I'd go around, and after you'd been sat there for a few minutes, you knew what would be coming.

'Bored?' she'd say, giving you a squinty look.

'No, Auntie,' I'd reply quickly. But no matter what you answered the result was the same. She'd hand you a newspapers, scissors and some string.

'Here, cut this up then and put it on the string,' she'd say.

And that was you making the toilet paper because we didn't have tissue then like you have today. Terrible when you think about it. You'd end up with this awful dirty, inky bum. It made you only ever want to do a wee!

That aunt had an outside toilet as well. If you lived in a house, the toilet was nearly always outside. Although at least they flushed – by then there was a proper running sewage system under the ground. I don't suppose it was too bad going in the daytime in the summer, but when it was cold in the winter . . . and needing the toilet at night when you were staying somewhere with an outside toilet was the worst! You would do anything to hold it in. Walking out there in the dark and cold . . . oh, it was awful.

I don't remember using toilet paper until my late

teens, and even then it wasn't like you have today. It wasn't on a roll, but came in a packet, in the way you have a box of tissues. There would be a slit in the side of the box where you would take out a few sheets to use. It was seen as a luxury at first, and then became more of a day-to-day thing.

I did have one doll that I think I must have got from Clara Grant – and can you believe Dolly was her name . . . very original I know! She had a painted china head and a cloth body. I used to undress and bath her, then wash her clothes and put them back on. Then I'd knit little outfits for her.

I managed to get a pram, I can't remember where from, probably one of the older girls in Bilberry House had outgrown playing with it. And I'd wheel Dolly up and down, up and down, along the landing, as proud as could be, like, pretending I was a mum taking her daughter out for a trip.

I had that doll for years. She was the one toy that really played a part in my life. When I was about ten, though, I remember someone, maybe one of the boys in the area, if I'm not mistaken, swinging her at a wall and she smashed. Her head broke into pieces. Oh, I cried my eyes out at the time and had to be comforted by my mum. She was my favourite toy! But I didn't keep her after that. I knew she couldn't be mended so I just threw her in the bin. And as with most things as a child, she was soon forgotten.

We also had an old deck of cards that we played with. Not that we really knew how to play many games. It was mostly messing around, or playing snap and the likes. And there was a snakes and ladders board that we got hold of that gave us hours of entertainment.

I'd sometimes play with my brother. He was a lovely happy-go-lucky boy, and protective of me, as boys are. We were close growing up, he was great. Of course we rowed, as you do when you are brother and sister, but it never got physical. I just used to get upset.

'Everyone's on at me, no one loves me any more!' I'd sob.

'No, don't cry, Pat,' he'd say, immediately giving in!

He used to get a couple of comics each week that we would sit and look at together. They were *Beano* and *Dandy*. I don't remember there ever being one for girls. If we were really lucky, sometimes at Christmas he'd get the annual, you know, the book. But other than that we didn't go in for reading of any kind really.

I don't remember being that creative neither, or making up games, or role playing cowboys and Indians, or doctors and nurses, or whatever those kind of games are. Plus we weren't allowed far enough from the flat to allow for that much exploring or adventures. As a kid I was only really allowed in the flat, along the landing, and on the open area in front of the flat that was enclosed by the buildings on each side of it. For whatever reason, my parents worried a lot more than most about what I'd get up to, or what would happen to me. And it meant that my boundaries were so restricted it sometimes felt it was hardly worth going out the front door. Not that Tommy had it so tough – as a boy, and I suppose because he was older, he seemed to be allowed to head out and roam just about anywhere. 'How unfair!' I used to think.

So instead I spent a lot of time listening to the wireless. Radio in them days is what telly is today. It was like your lifeline to the outside world, and a source of a lot of your entertainment.

Our radio was this great big box – more like the size of a small TV today. And it just had these two dials, one to tune it in, and one for the volume. It was such a hard task getting it tuned in perfectly – or as perfectly as possible – to a channel, that me and my brother weren't allowed to touch it. 'Don't muck about with it in case you break it!' and all that. So it was always set to a channel called the Home Service. I think Radio Luxembourg was also transmitting at this time, but unless there was something my dad especially wanted to hear on it, no one dared change it over.

The show that I remember most was *Appointment with Fear*, narrated by The Man in Black. It was scary stories told one evening a week, and oh, it frightened the life out of you. We'd all be sitting there in the front room – my mum and dad, Tommy and me – listening to it, frightening ourselves over it. I'd be huddled in the chair all like 'I'm scared! I want to go to bed!' but somehow enjoying it too. Sometimes you'd be doing another job at the same time, like sewing, but mostly we would be giving our full attention to the radio – and, of course, as soon as it was over, despite being so terrified, I couldn't wait until the next show was on. And I think my parents enjoyed it as much as us kids. They certainly made sure they were sat by the radio as it was about to start each time anyhow!

One of my happiest memories ever from when I was a kid was hop picking in Kent. This was a real East End tradition that most families got involved with, and we did this every summer for six weeks in our school holidays, from as young as I can remember, to when I was about thirteen. That was the only holiday I ever had as a kid, but I'm not complaining, I loved it. We all enjoyed it. And anyway, you came back brown as a berry with this nice colour like you'd been abroad. But going abroad wasn't a normal thing then, or least not for working-class people. It wasn't even an option or something you thought about or dreamed of – it was just so far out of reach you didn't even think about it.

No, it was hop picking for us, and that was great. It was like a big summer camp for families – although with a lot more work involved! Mainly mums and their children, but the odd dad would be there, if he wasn't working at the time, or if he'd got time off to come down as well. All my aunts and cousins would be there too, and friends from school – even my nan would be down there, and had been hop picking long before I was born, as she liked to tell me!

Everyone would go straightaway, as soon as the summer holidays started, to a meeting place, where we'd be picked up by lorry. Health and safety and all that would have a field day today, but then it was the way to go. We'd all be bundled in with our suitcases – or tea chests. Them days you didn't have proper suitcases, you had these big box tea chests with everything in them, and your name stuck on top so people knew whose they were. Then everyone would be sat on the cases or the floor, and we'd be bumping our way along down to Kent, all singing, and going along, and having a glorious time.

Once there, you would spend your days working your way along the rows of vines in the fields, picking the hops. You had to pull the vine down and run your fingers along it to get the leaves off. And you'd put them in a bin, a great big long bin. And then you had white flowers, and that is the bit they wanted. Like the bit that is used to make beer, so you put those into a different basket thing.

Then these two fellows would come around to collect your work. One fellow would lift the hops out, fill his arms up and put what you had got into a sack. Then they'd sew the sack up and write your number on to it. You'd all have a number, and it would be on your bin too. And then they'd weigh it, and you would be paid for the amount you had collected. You weren't paid daily, though, weekly I think it were that my mum and me went and picked up our pay.

It was tough work, and you ended up with sore fingers, all covered in this green stuff from the vines. But it was great fun. I think partly because it was something different to our usual life in London. And also it was the only time we got to go out to the countryside. It was a really nice area, and from what I can remember, the sun was always shining. It might be my kid's memory putting a spin on it, but back then it seemed like you got proper summers, not like today. Then you'd get sunshine in summer, and cold and snow in winter. Everything in its right season.

Anyway, we'd stay in these little wooden huts at night that ran right the way along the field. They were pretty basic little places. There was a wooden base in them for your bed, with straw on it to make it softer, and you covered it with sheets and slept on it. And there were no toilets in the huts – for that you had to trek across a field to this temporary wooden hut, newspaper cuttings in hand. Inside you sat on this plank of wood with a circular hole cut in it, with a hole in the ground underneath that the farmer had dug, and did your business.

Every night the farmer would come round and pour this white powder down, lime I think it was, to kill off the germs, then he'd add more dirt and dig it over. If it wasn't too late in the evening I liked to watch, and see the smoke and steam coming up.

After a few years the holes in the soil were replaced with buckets that the farmer could just change every night. Still pretty basic, though!

As for eating, well outside the hut where we lived was this big open fire which you kept burning all the time with faggots – the name we used for bundles of wood that burned well. Over the fire you had two metal rods stuck into the ground at either side, and a third one lying across from one to the other, with hooks on. These were so you could put a kettle and your saucepans on them and do your cooking over the fire. You'd keep water boiling all day long so you could go and get a cup of tea, or cook dinner. You could only ever boil anything mind, so there were no big roast dinners. It would be a stew or boiled chicken with boiled potatoes and carrots most nights. Then we could play around outside as we wanted after dinner. But more often than not you were too tired, and just wanted to go to sleep.

After the war Dad was able to come down with us, but I remember when he was still in the Navy he might just come and visit us for a day. I remember twice he landed at Portsmouth and came up to Kent for a visit, and then he stayed longer than he should have. He thought, 'I'll have another night off from the Navy.' I didn't know how it worked by law and was just pleased he'd stayed, and could see it made my mum happy. The first time, he got away with it, but the second time, well, he was expected back on his ship and didn't go, so he was considered a deserter. And don't you know it, the police came and arrested him. He got a fine, as I remember. So it wasn't great, but he didn't have to go to jail or anything.

Those trips were also a good thing for my mum 'cause we couldn't afford a holiday, but it was like we were getting one and actually earning money at the same time. My mum used to take all the money, of course – we were too young to see any of it ourselves – but we'd get treated with things as a well done, mainly, I think, by having the money used for our Christmas. Mum would save it up to one side, so that when it got later in the year she could afford to buy me and Tommy presents, and a nice Christmas dinner, because without that money set aside, I don't think we could have really afforded to do much.

Our Christmases were the kind of Christmases you know today, but also not – they were a lot more traditional and a lot less extravagant – you just wouldn't have had the money for it. So presents were practical like, more than anything.

Me and my brother didn't have stockings, but we'd hang up a pillowcase before bed. Not that we got much in it, I'll tell ya! There was the traditional stuff like an orange, an apple and nuts. Then you might get socks, slippers, pyjamas and a writing book, something like that. I suppose they couldn't do it no other way, than to dress up the things that really were a necessity, as though it was a treat. We didn't buy anything for each other as kids – I had no money of my own then, as pocket money was unheard of, so my mum and dad didn't expect anything from us.

For food you would have turkey, like you do now. Now you can have it every day of the week, but then you only ever got it for Christmas, so it was a real treat. Then the fruit, it was the same for that, you only ever got all those different fruits at Christmas time, whereas they are out in the supermarkets every day of the year now. The food would start coming in the shops in about November, and you'd be like, 'Ooh, it's nearly Christmas!' and feel the excitement starting for all the luxury you were going to get. For me it was much more special then.

EIGHT

Pea Soup

The downside of Christmas is it did get extremely cold, like chill you to the bones, get inside your coat, make your toes too icy to sleep, that kind of cold! In fact over the whole of the winter months it was the same, so I was right glad of our open fire. It was in the front room so that was always the room you wanted to be in. The other rooms didn't have fires.

There were three main things we used to keep the fire going, 'cause you wanted it going twenty-four hours a day when you were home in those months. It might die down overnight, and then you'd stoke it up in the morning, but it rarely went completely out. It was too cold! But yeah, the three things were coal, coke and tarry blocks.

Coal was like the poshest – and most expensive – of the three options. Although it didn't burn up and get as hot as coke, it lasted much longer. Once a week, every Friday I think it was, the coal man would come round in this great big lorry, with all these bags of coal on the back. And he'd shout out, 'Coal! Anyone for coal!' and if you wanted some you had to race down – or if you were feeling lazy, shout from the balcony, and he'd bring it up to you. He'd carry this big heavy bag of coals over one shoulder up the stairs and right to your door. Then that would go in this wooden box in the kitchen with a door on the front, where you would store it until you needed it. Then other than that there was a coal bucket next to the fire which you would top up, so it was close at hand.

Obviously, we only kept the coal in the kitchen 'cause we were in a flat – if you were in a house it would be out in the garden or garage. Besides, it wasn't often we could afford it, coal was a luxury.

So the next cheapest option was coke. And getting that for the fire was my and my brother Tommy's job. Coke was like a cheaper coal. It looked grey and had holes in it that you could see through, but it was still hard, and would burn up more. So this was something everyone had to buy back then.

Every Saturday me and Tommy would head to what they called the coke yard down St Paul's Way, about half a mile away. They made the coke in the factory next to it, the Gas Works. They'd burn coal to get gas, and coke was what got left over. I remember the men who worked in there 'cause they wore clogs. I've no idea why!

Anyway, you'd go down armed with a sack and a pram we kept just for this purpose. You'd see all the other locals heading down there too with anything they had with wheels: old prams, pushchairs, things they had fashioned themselves to make the journey, that could carry the sack back for them basically.

Then at the yard you'd fill up in the outdoors bit for tenpence a helping – a good shovel full. It was pretty dirty and grimy there, and I remember the air was kind of grey and weirdly dusty.

And you'd charge people back at the flats to get coke for them. Like old people, who didn't want to be bothered going down themselves.

'Off to the coke yard?' they'd say. ''Ere get us a sack full while you're there.'

'Ok then,' you'd agree, and they'd hand over their sack to you 'cause you had to bring your own one down – they didn't give you one there.

I always enjoyed going to the yard. It wasn't like a job, more of an outing, like an adventure, where I had a valid reason to be allowed further than usual from the flat. My brother would be pushing the pram with me walking alongside him, holding on to it. Then when you got back you'd tell the old neighbours you'd put two lots in the bag when you hadn't, you'd have put in one. But people would believe you, so you'd get more money. Or you'd fill it up for two shillings, but tell them it was half a crown – two shillings and sixpence like.

We didn't feel guilty – everyone used to do it, and besides, we'd done all the work! You didn't get pocket money in them days, so this was the closest I had to getting that. Not that I had anything to actually spend it on. There wasn't all kids' stuff that you could just go out and buy, you would never think of just going off and spending it. So mostly I'd just save it, and maybe give it to my dad to add to the money for clothes next time someone did take me shopping. And, of course, I could take my farthing out of it to pay my way when I went to Clara Grant each week!

But the cheapest option of all, cheaper than coal or coke, was tarry blocks. They were these wooden blocks with tar over them, which smelt awful and caused a lot of smoke, but they kept the fire burning, lasted all night, and were cheap – which is all that was important to most folks then. Well, I say cheap, but the reality is that the set price of them was still dear for the likes of us to fork out on. But in fact, if I'm honest, I considered them cheap because most of the time they were free!

Now don't judge me on this because everyone was

at it, but basically the blocks were originally used for paving the road. These blocks were laid into the road, but they were good for fires too. So you'd, erm, find out where the latest road works were going on, and go down and help yourself to the old ones as they were dug up. Or sometimes people went down at night and nicked the new ones that were laid out ready for the next day's work! I even saw people digging them up out of the road when times were especially hard and there were no road-works happening!

Most of the time it wouldn't have been me off getting the blocks, though, as it was seen mainly as a boy's job. So either Tommy or my dad would bring them home. You didn't need a lot – one block would keep burning through a night and a day. They're big thick things that would just keep burn, burn, burning. Ask anyone who lived in the East End of London at that time, and if they are honest, they will tell you they did exactly the same to get those blocks!

There was one major problem caused by these house fires, though – smog. Oh, the smog and the smoke was terrible. It would descend down on London like nothing you have ever seen. It was this dreadful thick black, absolute thick black, that you just couldn't seem to escape or get out of. It stopped you breathing and, basically, being able to live a normal life.

From what I understood, it was caused by a mix of smoke from the factory chimneys, and the smoke from people's fires. The combined smoke would build up over the city, and I suppose if there wasn't much wind to move it on, it just kind of settled like.

You would wake up in the morning and look outside, and it would have settled overnight, and you couldn't see. We'd still go to school but we'd be shuffling along the pavement holding hands, feeling our way with our feet. Traffic would all but stop because no one could see to drive, and buses wouldn't run, or if they did, a conductor would walk in front carrying a lantern as they drove to check the way. That's how bad it was, it was terrible.

You couldn't catch your breath – it got really caught in your lungs – and people with chest problems were dying because of it. No one I knew closely, but you would hear about it. So people would try walking with a hanky or something covering their mouths, but within minutes it would be covered in this thick black dust. And it got in your clothes, your hair . . . everywhere. It was really bad. You couldn't get away from the smell neither. It was this smoky, tarry smell that got right in your lungs.

We used to call it the foggy time when the pea soup settled in. That's what people used to say, 'Oh no, the old pea soup is coming down again now'. For that was its nickname, 'cause it had this thick impenetrable feel and sometimes it would have like a yellowy green colour to it.

It would only ever get like that in January or February – the coldest months – and sometimes it might just last a day and then clear up, or sometimes it was on and off for weeks, at night as well as day. Never in summer, though.

Things started to improve, I suppose, as factories cut down on their fires, and also people switched from big open fires in their homes to central heating over the coming years.

NINE

Losing Mum

I was twelve when my life was changed for ever. And I never saw it coming.

It was just a normal evening in April 1948. We had had dinner and I said 'Goodnight Mum, Goodnight Dad' and we all went off to bed. Then in the middle of the night I got woken up by one of my aunties.

'Come on, love, get up quick,' she said as I blinked at her. 'You must come over to me.' Tommy was already up and we stumbled along the balcony to her flat and then just sat there, curled up, miserable and tired, with no real idea of what was going on. I suppose I must have fallen asleep and dozed on and off for the next few hours.

From what I could find out later from my dad, Mum was taken ill in the night, and one of the neighbours was sent to the police box to get help. In them days you didn't have phones, but you had these boxes on most street corners that let you call through to the emergency services. They were like old metal boxes with a light on the top to attract attention, and they had a dial on the front so you could call through for whatever help you needed. There was one number for the police, one for ambulance, and one for fire.

So someone ran to the box and put a call out, then an ambulance came and she was taken off to hospital. But I was at this aunt's house the whole time, and had no idea what was going on.

The only way you got news then of what was happening at the hospital was through a telegram. It was never good news to see a telegram boy in the flats. We'd always gasp when we saw one arrive on his bike. They were mostly teenage boys, about fourteen or fifteen years old, all dressed in their little suits, wearing hats and carrying a telegram on yellow paper. And whoever's flat they were heading to, we'd know someone was ill or dead 'cause that's the only news you ever had from those telegrams. Sending a telegram was expensive, so it wasn't the kind of thing you would send with just some light-hearted news or for someone's birthday or whatever, unless you were rich, and no one around our area was.

So when one of those telegram boys turned up almost as soon as Mum arrived at the hospital, Dad must have known.

The telegram told him she had died of rheumatic heart and kidney trouble.

As far as I know she hadn't been ill – or if she was it wasn't something she shared with us kids. But maybe she never mentioned anything 'cause she didn't realize herself. Although sometimes I do look back at old photos from then and think, 'You did not look well, Mum'. So I guess there was something going on. It's not normal to die at just thirty-five anyhow, is it? It still gets to me, if I think about it too much, even now.

Anyway, after my mum died, Dad sat us down, me and Tommy, in our front room. I felt scared as I looked at Dad's face. He took a deep breath and said, 'Mummy has gone to see the angels up in heaven.' I remember his voice trembling as he said it, and me and Tommy just looking at him, struggling to take it in. I can't really remember, but I'm not sure I cried until later. I remember neighbours calling round, and talking quietly to my dad, and my nan being there, trying to help out and organize things. There was just a sense of shock in our house. I knew life was never going to be the same. And I just wanted my mum.

But that one conversation with my dad was it. We didn't talk about her dying again. You just got on with life. You got on with everything.

Although, of course, first there was her funeral. There

was a church service with family, friends and all that. I don't remember too much about the service, I think I protected my mind a bit by shutting off, but I do know I looked around at everyone who had come along to say goodbye to her, including my ol' Nan Polly, and thought how strange it is how death takes some people so young.

Then we drove to Bow Cemetery – or Tower Hamlets Cemetery as it's officially called – for the burial, but when we arrived I was told not to get out of the car. Tommy did, but they said I wasn't allowed to go to this bit of her funeral because 'it'll play on your mind to see your mum's coffin go into the ground'. That's how you did it in them days, they were trying to protect you. It was a different way of thinking – today anyone of any age goes to these things, babies and everyone.

But – and no one knows this until now – I did go to watch her be buried. I got out of the car after they had left me, and went to have a look. Something inside me made me want to see what was happening to my mum, and I watched it from a distance. No one realized I was there, but I did see her coffin go into the ground, and the vicar talking, and I don't think it affected me any more badly than it already was doing, so I was glad I had done it. Then when they all started coming back,

I ran and was back in the car before they saw I had been out.

I went to live with an auntie down the hall for a short while, I suppose while my dad got his head together, and then I was moved on to some other aunts here and there until he was recovered and ready to look after me again. Tommy stayed at home, though – I suppose it was seen that he was old enough to look out for himself. Maybe also, as a boy, he wasn't seen as needing an older female around in the same way as I was.

At that point my dad said, 'Oh, let her come home', and I was back at the house, although people still checked on us a lot for a while. Them days people came to help you. They'd pop round and say, 'Oh, I'll do this for you, I'll look after her, I'll do a bit of washing', that kind of thing. They'd just pop in because there would be a key behind the letterbox to get in, although most of the time the door was open anyway. Especially because by then my dad had taken on a night shift as well as his job in the day, I suppose 'cause he had to pay for everything on his own, now we didn't have money from my mum's job, so often he was away overnight and they'd check up on me. The only thing was, it was always just practical help that was offered, and I suppose what I was needing then was some kind of emotional support, someone I could talk to, who could be a mum, really. I wanted a mum, I needed someone like her there for me that next year to comfort me. 'Cause after her death, life just wasn't the same.

I loved my brother to bits, but he wasn't much use when it came to that. Sometimes I used to go to bed and cry my eyeballs out, night after night. Tommy was in the same room, and he'd say, 'Shut up, what's wrong with you?', not knowing what was going through my mind.

Of course he was very upset too, he loved Mum, but you didn't show your feelings – you couldn't tell anybody these things in them days, you just had to deal with it yourself. So he would have been annoyed with me that I wasn't and, I suppose, he didn't understand how to deal with it.

If I'm really honest, I wished Tommy had been a sister instead. I loved my brother to death, but I've always thought if he'd been a girl, and I'd had a big sister, I would have loved to have had that. Someone that I could have talked with about girls' things, got advice from, spoken to about what was going on, and all that. It's maybe been the hardest point in my life not having that female to talk to, without a mother or a sister.

Sometimes I did try and talk to some of the local women who came to help about things. But their own children didn't like it. I remember going to one woman a few times for help, like if I felt ill or had a pain, and her daughter not being happy about it. Like one time I went round and said, 'Is your mum in? I've got a headache and need her help.' And she said to me, 'She's not your mum so you can't ask that. She ain't your mum, she's just an auntie.' It was upsetting, but you know girls can get bitchy, and they did say to me when they were older, 'Oh, we didn't mean it!' but by then the time had passed and it was in my mind not to ask too much for help.

Even when I was having a hard time in school, I had no one to talk to about it.

I had swapped to my senior school when I was eleven, in the summer of 1947, the year before Mum died. I left Devons Road School and went to Southern Grove School – an all girls' school that later changed its name to the Elizabeth Barrett Browning School.

We had a school uniform, and the style was a bit like St Trinian girls. Like those gym slips. It was black with a pleat and a sash on it, and you wore it over a white blouse or top. I can't say I especially enjoyed that school either, though.

As a kid, my ginger hair wasn't really a big thing – people didn't make fun of it, like sometimes seems to happen to ginger kids now. If anything, it was a bit different, but it was just a fact, not something to be mocked. Where I did get teased, though, was for my freckles. Oh, I used to have so many freckles all over my face, and under my eyes, and everywhere! And I'd go to school and the kids would start making fun of me for it.

'Fly shit face,' they used to say to me. 'The flies have landed on you, and look what they've done!'

I'd go home from school at the end of the day and cry my eyes out. And I wanted someone to tell about it. 'They called me fly shit face, Mum!' But of course there was no one to say it to. So instead I'd go into the toilet and get a cloth and try and scrub at my face. I used to think I could get them off if I did it enough. And I'd be there scrubbing away, and hoping against hope that they were fading, until I'd convinced myself they'd faded a bit, and I'd keep going. Instead all I ended up with was a red and damaged face!

But maybe it did work 'cause actually they did fade as I got older, and now I don't really have any! But at the time, I wish I'd had someone to talk to about it. Although it was only kids having a laugh and a joke, you sometimes need an adult to put that straight for you and reassure you that you look pretty anyway.

But I don't want to sound like I was totally alone. I did have a few aunties that I turned to more than others. One of my favourite aunts was a real one, Mary. She was my dad's sister, and was very glamorous and stylish in my eyes. She was very proper and wouldn't leave home without a hat and a pair of gloves on – even if she was just nipping down the shop for a loaf of bread or something, the full outfit would go on. Real lady she was.

I didn't have a specific one who became like a surrogate mum, though. They all had their own lives to be leading and own kids to look after, and while I did go to different ones for different bits of advice, they were never more than aunties.

I got used to being independent minded and working things out for myself. It wasn't always easy at all, and I was lonely and frightened a lot, if I am honest, but I think it made me get quite strong too. I think I can ride through most things mentally. You just do what you have to do.

What I was lacking was someone to talk to me about the biological things that a mother would tell their daughter. Just life stuff, the birds and the bees and that. I remember it was my nan – ol' Poll – who told me about periods. I was about thirteen when mine started, but I remember she sat me down a few months before that to tell me about it. And I mean good on her for taking on that role and discussing it with me, 'cause I am sure she wasn't comfortable with it. But, oh, the way she described it I was expecting floods and floods of blood to come, you know, so I was quite terrified about it. And she really made me feel like it was a shameful thing to be going through.

And some of the other things she used to drum into my head . . . they were hardly a step forward for society I don't think! She used to say to me, 'Don't go out of the door when you've . . .' Well, they never called it the period, they used to call it by all sorts of names. Anything but that word really. Anything that totally avoided mentioning it, if you know what I mean – I wouldn't have dared because that would have been shameful. I think I mostly just said 'the time of the month' to refer to it.

'Always wear black knickers when it is that time,' my nan told me. 'And don't let your brother see what's going on.'

And she got me these sanitary towels. You know, great big thick ones with a sanitary belt that you had to wear then. It was like an elastic belt that went around you with a hook on the front and a hook on the back. Then you would get this big thick sanitary towel and hook it on. Oh, they were terrible. All big and uncomfortable, you couldn't forget when you were wearing one. Not like the tiny little simple things you get today.

Anyway, that was the women in my life, but I also had some male family friends, and although they got less involved – kept themselves more separate in them days did the men – they were still uncles to me. And actually, if I worked it out, I had plenty of real ones of them too. My dad was one of eleven boys – minus the ones killed in the war – so that left a lot of uncles to choose from, not to mention all the ones half removed, or what have you, that made up half the Spicers dotted around East London.

But do you know the thing I loved about them most was their names. I swear I don't know what went through my ol' Nan's head when she named them. Then again, I suppose coming up with eleven boys' names that you actually liked wasn't that easy. She had Bobby, and Harry, and Elbert and Kitchener . . . but when she got to the eleventh boy she ran out of ideas. So she went back to her favourite name Bobby, and said she wanted to name him that. But instead she doubled it, so she went, 'I'll name him Bobby Bobby.' No word of a lie! I'll never forget that. It was so funny. Every time we saw him we couldn't help but bring it up, 'Hello Uncle Bobby Bobby!' and laugh. And he'd always shake his head and look glum and just say, 'I can't believe my mother!' Honest to God, it was funny.

I guess looking back, everyone did try and make my life continue as normally as possible. Like in the school holidays for example, my nan took me hop picking for a couple of years after my mum died. By then Tommy had stopped coming as he had to work. But all my cousins and aunties would go too.

But then Nan died. I was only about fourteen at the time. I don't remember what she died of, but it was horrible, especially so soon after my mum. I felt I was really just coming to terms with losing her, when the other main woman in my life died.

And while he never talked about it, I'm sure my dad must have been suffering. To lose your mum after your wife . . . but it wasn't his way to discuss it. And she was buried and we got on with our lives.

As for hop picking, well, I never went no more. It has died out since then, though. I think after a while machinery took over the job that we were doing, and then lager took over from beer in popularity so less hops were needed anyway.

Dad seemed to change after Mum died and he definitely changed the way he treated us kids. He became a lot stricter and a lot more bossy and domineering. I think it was just his way of trying to be protective, and I guess I understand it, but it was tough to live with at the time. I suppose for him, when my mum was alive she was the parent who was kind of guiding us through life, and Dad was happy to sit back and let her take that role. But without her around, it was like he felt it was now down to him to step up and do that. So instead of playing the laid-back father role, he started laying down the law, telling us how things were to be done, and disciplining us if they weren't. But I suppose he just stepped up a bit too much and went over the top. Don't get me wrong, he never laid a finger on us, but he would just shout, and have strict rules. You know that kid who is never allowed to venture as far as her friends, or who has to be the first in of a night? Well, that was me back then.

TEN

Head of the Household

Weirdly, although in some ways my dad's strictness meant I was treated very much like a child, there were some huge changes in my life that meant I suddenly had to become like a grown woman. Once I was living back home, it was left to me as the only female in the house to deal with the day-to-day running of it, in particular all the housework. My dad and brother helped out the first few times, just to make sure I'd got the hang of it, but then, at twelve years old, it became my role to look after them. Kids now would never do it, would they? But I never questioned it. It's just the way things were, a woman was needed to do all that stuff in the house, so that's how it went from then on, and I got on with it.

I'd get occasional help from one of my aunts, or different women in the block – there was one lady along the landing I remember who used to pop her head in and say, 'Let me give you a hand with that, Pat' – but ultimately it was for me to do. Which at that age was a fair bit of responsibility on pretty young shoulders. Most girls my age were starting to help their mums out, not totally run the house.

It's perhaps yet another reason that school wasn't important to me – I had enough on my plate. If I'm honest I didn't bother with secondary school that much. I hadn't been there long when Mum died, then between the funeral and moving in with aunts I missed out on quite a lot. When I did go back my attendance was pretty on and off to tell the truth. I went when I could fit it in with my housework and when it suited and no one really chased up to see where I was, so it worked out fine. And looking back, I don't think I had a choice, and I don't regret it – it was the right thing to do.

The only thing I maybe regret is that I can't read better, although it wasn't such a big thing then. My reading skills are enough to get me by, but I'm a bad reader really. I'm not a 100 per cent at it, and I would like to be better, and sometimes it embarrasses me that I'm not. So I don't think I learned a lot from Southern Grove. And I can't really remember much about it.

Years on, I came across the Kray Twins – although the details of that story are for my next book – but someone told me they had gone to Southern Grove and were there two years ahead of me. But again, I probably wasn't there enough to have even come across them. I don't remember seeing them at school anyhow.

Back then, each kind of housework had its set day. So everyone in the area would be on the same task at the same time. Today people are doing it every minute of every day, but not then.

So Monday was washing day, ironing was Tuesday, Wednesday was cleaning and all that business, and food shopping, well, that was pretty much every day. So on wash day, you'd change the beds and wash everything on a rubbing board. It took time, and it wasn't easy – there were none of these washing machines or tumble dryers then to make life easier. But how it worked was our bath was in the kitchen, as I've said earlier.

You lifted up the wooden top and there was the bath. Next to it was a boiler, like a big cylinder that you put bits of wood underneath to light a small fire, to get the water to come to the boil. Then you'd turn this little tap on the side of it to let the water into the bath – although never all of it mind 'cause you didn't want the fire to burn the inside of the boiler. Then you'd be in trouble!

And you would add what we called 'the special powder' – washing powder really, but I tell you what, it did a lot more good at cleaning stuff than some of this fancy washing powder stuff these days. They're all about the advertising, and hardly about the cleaning!

You'd do your whites first. You'd put them in the bath and get the rubbing board and rub them up and down that until they got clean. It didn't half kill your back mind! Next you got your mangle, or your wringer – it was like two wooden rollers that you turned with a handle, and fed the clothes through, squashing them to wring them out – then hang them over the line so they'd get dry. The more water you could get out of them in the mangle the easier drying was. And if you did it enough it would make them smooth and you could avoid ironing them. So with sheets and pillowcases, you'd wring them, fold them smaller, wring them, fold them smaller, wring them. Then finally hang them up to dry.

If it was a lovely sunny day you would hang them out to dry on lines that were set up in the courtyard in front of our flat. And if it weren't good weather, I used to get things dry by putting them on a rail that went up on the ceiling in the flat, on a pulley line. So you'd pull a string to get it up and down, and it would go in a zigzag formation across the ceiling. Then all the clothes would be drip, drip, dripping away, and if you needed to pass by, you had to duck your head or you'd be wringing wet too! But it would mostly be dry by the next morning.

Meantime, the water in the bath would have cooled down, and you could go through the process all over again with your coloured clothes.

Once a fortnight you got the curtains down and they got a wash too. It was a regular thing. You're lucky if most people's curtains ever see washing powder these days!

The whole thing generally took the best part of a day for most people, although it depended on the size of your family. Because we were just the three of us, and then later when Tommy left home, just the two, my washing days weren't too bad. I would sometimes fit it in after school – I finished mid-afternoon, so I'd have the rest of the day to do it. Or sometimes I skipped school to keep up with it, but you didn't have so many clothes to wash as today, as you didn't automatically wash everything. You had to learn as you took it off each night to decide whether it was dirty or smelly, and if it wasn't – well, then you just kept it and wore it again the next day. And the next as well if it was still fine to wear.

No, with my small load to wash, it was more Mrs Armitage upstairs with her thirteen kids that I felt sorry for! She did get the grandmother and eldest kids to help out, but still.

So that was Mondays, then Tuesday it was on with ironing anything that needed it. There were two types of iron I remember using at the time. There was the iron iron, called that, as I suppose you can guess, because it was made of cast iron! It was a great big thing that sat in the corner of the fireplace so it was always hot. You couldn't put it direct on the clothes – it would burn or stain them, and make it ten times worse than just having a few creases. No, you had to put a sheet or something over the clothes and then iron over the top of that.

Then the other iron I had was the electric one. The light bulb would be hanging from the ceiling on its wire. You'd take out the bulb and plug the iron into this socket and it would heat up, and you would stand and do your ironing on a table or shelf, or sometimes the floor – there were no ironing boards in them days.

Then Wednesday was the day you cleaned your house. It meant giving all the surfaces a good scrubbing down. You didn't have a Hoover then, you swept up with a brush on the hard surfaces, and where there were carpets, you had one of them carpet cleaners called a Ewbank. I still had one until a couple of months ago! An old red one that had belonged to my dad, and I swear a lot of the time it was better than the job those Hoovers do.

As for food shopping, that was something that you did pretty much every day. The main reason was there were no fridges or freezers in them days so you didn't have a way to store things that would keep them for long. Instead, things were kept fresh on what we called cold slabs. They were like big tiles, and always felt cold to the touch, no matter where you had them sat. I think they were made of marble.

We had two cold slabs inside our cupboard. One was used to keep your bread and milk on, and the other was for butter and eggs. It gave you two or three days to keep the things fresh. Having said that, you just judged it by taste – there was no such thing as 'best before' dates in them days. You worked it out for yourself – and we never got sick that way, so it can't have been too bad!

The actual act of shopping back then was a completely different thing. The biggest difference was there were no supermarkets. And opening hours were totally different, they were much more reduced like. So on Sundays no one would have dreamed of opening up a store. I think it was illegal to tell the truth, but anyhow it was seen as a day for the family and of rest. Not that anyone around ours got much rest – not the women that is. The men might have been 'resting' in the pub, but the women would have been working at something or other. Back then shops weren't open on a Thursday afternoon. Thursday was half-day closing for years and years. And on a Saturday they'd close quite early, like about 4 p.m. I suppose that way it felt like they had a decent break through to Monday, before they had to open all over again.

All the shops were small, local family-run ones or market stalls that would specialize in one area, so you had to go to lots of shops to get your food. So for example, the baker only did bread and rolls – not even cakes or anything like that. And you'd pop in there for your fresh loaf of bread.

Then it was the butcher's for your meat. I remember the butcher's shop, with all the animals hanging up by their necks in the window on the hooks, the rabbits and the chickens. Quite gruesome, I suppose, for people today, but I think it was a good thing really. Least you knew it was fresh and you knew what you were eating! Not like now when it's all packaged and sanitized-looking, and you have no idea how long it has been dead for.

My favourite was a shop called Lovell's. That was the greengrocer's, and where you went for your potatoes and vegetables and that. And you may wonder why it was my favourite . . . well, I'd say it was the favourite shop of all the young girls, for we were all in love with the Lovells' son! Oh, he was lovely looking, but none of us ever got anywhere with him sadly.

Then there was Chrisp Street Market, but there wasn't all that amount of different things there. Much of it got destroyed in the war, so you didn't get many stalls there after that like. I think it has been developed since into a covered market, but at the time, it weren't too much use.

Once my mum had died and it was down to me to do the shopping and cooking, each night my dad would leave out so much on the kitchen table, and he'd say, 'Right, get tomorrow's dinner with this. I want such and such, and we'll have so and so.' Then that's what I'd do after school the next day – if I went. It was only dinner I made, though – he did his own toast in the morning for breakfast before work.

Or the other way you got your shopping done was by people coming to you. I can always remember this fella who used to come round in a van a couple of times a week. He'd have bread and cakes and hot pies, and he'd holler out to let you know he was there when he'd pulled up in the courtyard. He had a shop and he used to drive round and sell what he had left out of the van, I guess a bit cheaper like, at the end of the day.

You'd have to run down the stairs like mad when you heard his yell, and hope you made it before he went – he never hung around for long! But it was great – saved you having to work so hard to cook dinner.

Then there was the milkman. It's a shame the whole thing of milkmen seems to be dying out 'cause it was great to have him come around with the milk and eggs in his van. You'd wake up each morning and you'd have a fresh pint of milk waiting outside your door in a glass bottle with a silver foil top on it. Then that night when it was finished, you would put the bottle outside the door, and he'd take it away in the morning when he dropped off the new one. They would clean them out back at the factory, and just use them again.

So food each night was always fresh, but it was never anything too complicated, mostly a piece of meat with potatoes or vegetables. But I had never cooked with my mum before she had died. It wasn't like she had instructed me on how to make anything at all really – I don't suppose she had thought she needed to so early on, 'cause I suppose she thought she would be there to cook for the family for lots more years and she could have taught me when I was a bit older like. The most I had probably done was get a spoon and help out a bit when she was making cakes or something. Other than that I never did much cooking with her.

So yeah, I had to learn quickly. But that was just what I had to do, I had to get on with it. And I did get along. I got stuck into cooking on my stove in the kitchen, experimenting and learning by practice. I had a little gas stove in the kitchen, and an oven that was at the end of the open fire in the front room that was heated up by the warmth of the fire. You could keep things warm in there, or put a kettle or saucepan on top of it. It was a good little set-up, and I had fun trying things out and learning. Sometimes I liked the feeling that I was in charge of the house. Whereas most girls my age were playing at running a house, that was the reality of my life.

I asked one of my aunts in the flats if I got stuck, though, especially one called Aunt Dolly. She lived along the landing with her husband and two or three children, who were about my age, and who I'd played with sometimes before. But while they were still playing around, by then I had other things to think about.

She was a lovely kind lady, and if I didn't know how I was going to make what Dad had said he wanted, I'd go and ask her. 'How do you make so and so, Aunt Doll?' or how do you do this or that. And she'd show me. Or even better, nine times out of ten, bless her, she'd go, 'Well, funny enough I'm cooking that for our dinner tonight as well, so I'll bring you down some.' Then she'd show me how to do it for next time and send me home with some before my dad got back, so he'd think I'd made it all myself. That's how it would go 'cause everybody was in with one another in them days, not like they are now.

Then Sundays would be a Sunday roast at 3 p.m. Although not the extravagant affair it is now, with all the Yorkshires and ten types of veg and that. No, it was generally a bit of lamb and some potatoes. But always served at 3 p.m. on the dot!

Dinner was a much more formal affair in them days. There was none of this eating separately or when you felt like it, or eating off your lap in front of the TV. You would sit down at the table as a family, have your meal, wait until everyone had finished, clear away, then you had your afters – or your sweet/dessert – but we always called it afters. Though we should have just called it apple and something 'cause that's what it always was. Apples was easy and cheap to get hold of, so I always did something with them – apple crumble, stewed apple and custard, apple pie. Luckily we all liked apples!

Again, you would wait until everyone finished before you left the table, then I'd have to go and do the washing-up. No dishwashers in those days!

And of course I had to keep all the kitchen equipment in perfect working order. It wasn't like you could go and buy anything just because the old one was getting a bit blunt, or rickety or scratched. And that's where helpful people like the knife sharpener came in. He was one of my favourite of the door-to-door men, but you hardly see them no more. He'd come round with this grinder wheel in the basket on the front of his bike, and see if anyone needed knives or scissors sharpened.

You'd go down and queue up patiently to get your

knives done, just a couple of coppers a piece. And he'd be there, working away with his wheel spinning, then 'spit!', he'd spit on them as his grinder needed some wet to work best. More spinning and grinding, then *spit!* Oh, it's terrible really, but it worked a treat, and I always was fascinated watching him at work, and all the sparks flying off the knife, as it got shinier and sharper. You'd come away with these knives and scissors literally like new. Now, of course, when they go blunt you just get a new one.

The other person you used to see around the streets plying his trade was a chimney sweep. But he wasn't a common sight down our road, 'cause with us being in flats and sharing chimneys, and really not being that well off, it wasn't a place where he would find himself much needed.

But it was always good to see a chimney sweep going past on his bike, for they are a sign of good luck, or so I am told. They'd be passing with their long brushes strapped on to the side of their bikes, or balanced over one shoulder, and themselves covered head to foot in black. I don't know how they did it really. But those real old tradespeople were great. I'd pay good money to see them back out working the streets again.

ELEVEN

Hopscotch and Hot Cross Buns

Even though I had all these responsibilities at age twelve, it was still thought that I couldn't stay indoors in the house on my own of an evening. So if my brother was out and my dad wanted to go drinking, I had to go too.

He used to have a few places he liked to go – there were a lot of great East End pubs all within walking distance back then. Sadly a lot of them have been knocked down these days, or become run-down, or turned into chain pubs. But then, pubs really were the life and soul of the community – at least if you were a man, anyhow!

They were that well known and frequent, that people used to give directions by them. So it would be like, 'You want the church? Ok, well, go along this road until you get to The King's Head, then turn left. Walk along past The Nag, you'll see that, lovely place, and then turn right down the road opposite The Lion.' No word of a lie, that's how it went. Much more interesting than giving road names, eh, 'cause no one remembers those!

Anyway, his favourite was a pub called Kitsons – or later it changed to being called The Bricklayers Arms. You'd cut through our flats and be there in about two minutes – it was practically under the flats. These days it has changed names again – it is called The Liquor Inn, and I've no idea what it is like now, but it was popular in them days.

'Come on then, get ready, I'm off for a pint,' Dad would say after we'd had our dinner and I'd washed up. And I'd trot down there along with him. But children weren't allowed in the pub then. People forget that is how it used to be, but you would never have got these family friendly pubs then that you get now. Pubs weren't a place for women – they were supposed to be at home looking after the house – let alone children being allowed in there. It was a definite no under eighteens rule. They were real man's territory. Now you have babies in the bleedin' pub!

So instead, if it was a sunny evening, I was left to play out the front of the pub. Madness isn't it? I couldn't be left home alone, yet I could be left to play by myself by the side of the road in front of the pub. But you had no fear in them days, so I never thought about it.

Sometimes I might be the only kid there, but other times there might be half a dozen of us, girls and boys, taken down by the dads to entertain ourselves outside, while, well, while they entertained themselves inside. We'd wait around outside skipping, or playing hopscotch, or doing whatever, and they didn't care as long as we looked after ourselves.

If it rained I had to stand in the porch, or what they called the passageway that led into the bar. And I was given an arrowroot biscuit – and if Dad was feeling rich that day, a glass of lemonade as well. Oh, I can remember many the time I used to have to stand there with my arrowroot biscuit. They were these big biscuits that were like digestives that only cost about a penny or something. They were your pub staple food then, like, say, a packet of crisps might be today.

And standing in this passage I could see through to the bar, 'cause if I stood on my tiptoes, I could see over the top of the counter. I would stand and watch all that was going on in the pub. And I'd watch my dad drink his pint, and laugh and joke with the other men, and occasionally have a singsong. And every time someone opened the door there would be the smell of pipes, or cigars, or cigarettes wafting through, 'cause there was no smoking ban then of course, and everyone seemed to smoke. I don't suppose anyone knew it was bad for you then either.

Sometimes we'd try and sneak under the counter and go inside, but we'd always be spotted, and before we could get very far we'd hear, 'Oi, get out!' One of the dads or the landlord had seen us and that would be it. We were never politely asked to leave – it was always a very definite 'oi!' and we'd be sent scurrying on our way back out, giggling at our own cheekiness.

So that was the man's side of the bar, and it was called the Public Bar, but there was always a second room to the bar in those days, and the other one was called the Snug. This was a much more private bit where women were allowed to go, or, I suppose, anyone who didn't want to be seen in the Public Bar for whatever reason. But they'd mostly get the alcohol to take away to drink at home.

All these old women would arrive with their big pint jug and get it filled up in the Snug Bar for half a crown. 'I'll have a pint of so-and-so to take away, please.' Then they'd pick it up and walk home, and enjoy their drink in private. A lady hardly ever stayed in the bar them days. It's like you were allowed the alcohol, but not the social side. Although it was only ever the older women – the young women were too busy cooking, ironing, cleaning, sorting out the kids and keeping the house together to even think about stopping for a drink. No, that was a privilege saved for the older ones.

Oh, lots of old ladies were at it. I remember my nan, ol' Polly Spicer, was pretty partial to a pint of brown ale, and she'd often head down there on an evening, to get her jug filled up to take home.

As kids we'd be there running around the grounds, and if we saw an elderly person carrying a beer, we'd offer to help them carry it home. 'I'll help ya!' we'd call out, and we'd have a cheeky mouthful of the beer while we carried it.

Occasionally, men would get the takeaway beers too, if they weren't in the mood for being sociable. Not my dad, though – it was all about being sociable for him. I could see the pub was his place for relaxing so I didn't mind going down there with him. And looking back, I suppose, without my mum around it must have been pretty lonely for him at times of an evening.

Anyway, it was interesting to me too. Being nosey, it was better than sitting at home. It was the only way I got to play that far from the flat as well, without getting into trouble.

One of his other favourite pubs at the time was called The Widow's Son. It was a great wee pub, and is still there on Devons Road. I just hope it has kept hold of the atmosphere and tradition that it used to have. It was a real quirky place, full of navy and ship memorabilia. But the thing it was most famous for what it did on Good Friday.

According to local tale – and I can't guarantee this is true, but I can't see why it wouldn't be – a widow used to live on the spot where the pub now stands. One day back in the nineteenth century, her son went off to fight at sea in the war against Napoleon. She was expecting him home round Easter time, and decided to bake a hot cross bun for him 'specially to welcome him home.

Well, her son never did come home. But she kept the bun there for him, even when it went all stale and hard. Then the next year, when he still wasn't back, she made a second one and added it to the other one, and so on every year. Then, after she died, and the pub opened in place of her home, they decided to keep the tradition. So every year another bun is added to this huge net that used to hang over the ceiling with all the buns in it.

A funny tradition, but I haven't told you the best bit that kept me happy to trot along there with my dad on Good Friday – they gave a hot cross bun to every person in there to eat as well! So I'd be outside munching on mine. A nice change from the arrowroot biscuit . . . Oh, it didn't half get the people down there. I remember I used to look through the window and it would be packed solid with people. Nothing like a free bun to draw the crowds!

Years later when I was actually going to pubs myself I would still go back to that pub on a Good Friday, and it'd be filled with navy boys even then. There were sailors in uniform everywhere. And they love the attention, don't they . . . I always remember them saying to me, 'Touch my dicky bow, it will bring you luck!', meaning the white bit on their collar. Oh, the things they came out with them boys! But it worked. Everyone would go mad for them.

As far as I know that tradition in The Widow's Son is still going on today – imagine that, all them years later.

Then there was The Tenterden Arms, along Devons Road. I remember that place 'cause of the little steps it had outside the front. It was a nice looking pub, but it was the steps that mattered to me 'cause that's where I spent many an hour, waiting for my dad. There was a little metal railing that used to run down alongside the steps, and I'd spend ages sliding down it and spinning over the top of the bar.

Oh, he had a great ol' pub crawl going really, did my dad. All the places were within ten minutes from home, and he was well known in all of them. He definitely liked a drink did Dad, and I can't be forgetting that.

Although he did always know when to stop, I'll give him that. I don't remember having to help him walk home or anything. He was always capable of making his own way. And he always seemed cheerful enough. A night in the pub mostly raised his mood. I'm sure he was still missing Mum then as much as I was, but a night with friends seemed to do him good.

The only thing you were allowed into the pub for as a kid was to use the toilet. Mostly you tried to hold it in, or you might dash behind a tree or something, but a pub's public toilets really were the only ones you would ever think of using.

I remember there were public toilets in the street, but we were encouraged not to use them. They weren't exactly seen as good places, let's just say, so we were never ever allowed in them.

They used to be underground – there were a set of stairs running down into them, it kind of looked like the entrance to an underground station or something. It was men's toilets on one side and ladies on the other. But from what I understood, nine times out of ten, people didn't go to them to use the bathroom, they went to them to find a prostitute.

People would say, 'Don't you go down them toilets' with this knowing look, and then I found out later from friends in very hush hush gossip that it was 'the prostitutes what worked down there', 'girls after business', 'tarts with their bright red lipstick, working the street corners' or just 'girls who ain't no good'.

To be honest I didn't even really understand what a prostitute was. I actually thought, until years later when my husband corrected me, that it was just people showing themselves off to each other. I couldn't believe they would actually be having sex with complete strangers!

I even picked up a saying at that time that I innocently used for years after, just an old expression that I didn't realize had anything to do with prostitution. When someone used to ask me where I was going, if I couldn't be bothered to explain myself, I'd just say, 'Oh, I'm off to Piccadilly to earn myself a couple of bob.' I've always said it, and I don't know why, but it's just one of them things. I'm sure I picked it up off an aunt or someone along the way. An old East End saying, and I had no idea what I was actually telling people. Oops!

Around this time, Tommy left home. Me and him had shared a room the whole time growing up. We had the two single beds in there, and we both sort of looked after our own sides of the room. As we got older and wouldn't change in front of each other, it became a case of one of us running into the bedroom and changing first, and then the other going in. We never resented sharing a room, though – you never even imagined having one of your own really, that was a luxury, if you had brothers and sisters.

The only time I did get to have a room of my own was once he left home. He was still very young at the time, eighteen or nineteen, but he got married to a girl called Jeannie who he had been courting for a couple of years. She would come around our flat sometimes, although more often than not he went to hers over in Millwall where she lived with her parents. But once they were married they went off to set up their own home.

I don't doubt that one of the reasons he got married so early was to get away from my dad. Don't get me wrong, I did love Dad to bits, but he was so domineering – 'don't do this' and 'don't do that' all the time, it was pretty wearing on us as kids. I think my brother got it a bit easier – he was quieter and less argumentative than me. He tended to put his head down and get on with it, so he didn't really clash with Dad. He was more inclined to just go out to work – he turned his hand to anything that was going, and I remember he worked down the docks a lot – came home, had dinner, and did his own thing. He was quite a homely fella, and had a routine that was separate to my dad, and they didn't interfere too much with each other's lives. But I think getting married, moving out, and I guess showing his independence was pretty appealing to him all the same. And

Dad just accepted it when Tommy decided that was what he was going to do.

No, it was me, the daughter, who he was much more protective of. Like all men I guess, they worry about their daughters a lot more than their sons.

I remember Tommy's wedding mainly 'cause it was so cold! It was 22 March 1950 and there was thick snow on the ground at the time, and I was a bridesmaid, so standing there in my little pink taffeta bridesmaid dress in that weather was hardly the best. It was freezing! But it was a nice straightforward and simple family affair. It was in Millwall, where Jeannie was from, and after the ceremony we had a small reception in the church hall.

I forget where Tommy and Jeannie moved to first, but it was somewhere in East London. Then they moved around a fair bit, until they finally ended up in Millwall. I know that 'cause he was in East London it sounds like they were close, but he was always a fair bit away by standards in those days – more often than not people generally moved just down the street or round the corner from their families. So we didn't have so much contact after that, and I guess we weren't so close.

Not that I didn't want to be, but it wasn't so easy then. We didn't have phones, and my dad didn't have a car, so we couldn't just drive over to see them, and they didn't drive. There was the tube by then, but it would never even have come into my mind to use it. It would have been seen as too expensive, so I never got the tube as a kid.

It was strange after that, just me and my dad being in the house. Looking back I suppose it was a pretty lonely set-up for a teenage girl. But I was quite good in my own company by then, so I didn't mind too much. It was all I knew really, although I did used to look at Winnie and her big family sometimes, and envy the fact that she was always surrounded by people. She had a good family around her.

There is only so much conversation a teenage girl and her dad can have over the dinner table as well, especially in them days, when, as I said at the start, you didn't really talk about feelings or emotions with your parents, or anything deep at all.

We wouldn't have sat in total silence or anything, but it wasn't proper conversation. More like, 'How's your day been?', 'What do you want for dinner tomorrow?' 'Here, Auntie down the corridor is expecting a fourth kid', that kind of thing. Very surface-type conversations.

Around this time, when I was fourteen, Dad decided I didn't need to come down to the pub with him when he went, so I was allowed to stay in the house on my own in the evenings. Not that I had that much to amuse myself with. If I wasn't washing, ironing, knitting or

BOVE LEFT: Me as a toddler, around the age of two. You didn't take
any photos back then as hardly anyone owned a camera, so these old
ctures are very special to me.

BOVE RIGHT: Me as an evacuee in Derbyshire, with my favourite
erson there – the daughter of the woman who took me in.

BELOW: My dad's official Royal Navy photo. He is in the back row, right in the middle, looking very smart!

ABOVE: Me with Mum and Tommy when I was about eight, for a rare family photo. My mum looks so pretty here.

ABOVE: Didn't I have a cheeky grin for my official school photo! I was nine when this was taken.

LEFT: My nan, ol' Poll Spicer, all dressed up for a day out. She was an eccentric old lady who was deaf as a post, and I thought she was lovely.

IGHT: Clara Grant, the Bundle Woman f Bow.

ELOW: I swear the children waiting to see lara Grant were the only children in the vorld who were trying to get shorter rather han taller! Children would queue for hours o walk through the wooden arch and get ne of Clara's Farthing Bundles.

BELOW: Tommy, Mum and me snatching a moment's break while hop picking in Kent the summer before Mum died. It was a great holiday, but looking at my mum now, compared with the picture just a couple of years before, I can see that she wasn't well.

LEFT: Relaxing with two friends outside the cork factory where I got my first job. As always we were sat on the wall of a nearby house. I'd whipped off my turban for the photo!

BELOW LEFT: With another friend I made at the cork factory. I loved the independence that earning my own money brought me.

ABOVE RIGHT: This was one o the official photos taken outsid Bilberry House at our party for the Queen's Coronation. I am in the middle of the back row, with my hat at an angle. Winnie is standing to my left as you look at the picture, and he sister Gracie is beside her.

RIGHT: More Coronation celebrations. I am sat down at the far end of the table, helping out with the kids. Standing on the right is Mrs Armitage, Winnie and Gracie's mum, who always had her hands full looking after her thirteen children!

LEFT: My Charlie looking pleased as he walked to the church for our wedding day. Charlie was a tall, strapping fella, but he was still dwarfed by his brother – and best man – Dickie!

BELOW: My wedding day. As you look at the photo, the couple on the left are the mum-in-law and her boyfriend Joe, who gave me away. The couple on the right are my Aunt Alice – wearing her furs, of course – and her husband Stan. Then obviously in the middle are me and Charlie, Dickie, and our bridesmaids.

ABOVE: Me in my borrowed dress, which did me just fine. It was a lovely, happy day – although my dad and brother not being there did play on my mind.

RIGHT: There was no chance of honeymooning on our own on the Isle of Sheppey – Aunt Alice (not in the picture), Stan and their kids were just some of the people who 'happened' to show up! Everyone clearly liked any excuse for a holiday.

LEFT: The mum-in-law holding June when she was about eighteen months old.

BELOW: This was Stephen's christening – Charlie was over the moon that he finally had a boy! From the left is me, my dad, his partner Bet holding Stephen, Charlie's sister Mary, and in the front is June.

LEFT: Taking over The Rising Sun pub was the start of a new chapter in our lives. Exciting times!

sewing, I was mostly just listening to the wireless. But as I'd told him several times, I didn't need to be waiting outside the pub, I was old enough to stay home. So when he agreed, it was a sense of freedom and responsibility all the same, and a small victory for me!

TWELVE

Corks and Coronations

As you can imagine, the day I finished with school I was pretty happy. Even though I wasn't exactly going a lot, I didn't officially leave until fifteen which is the earliest you were allowed to. I had no qualifications – you didn't do exams in them days, like GCSEs or anything. I think you only did them if you were at private school.

So then it was a matter of getting on with finding a job. I had no career plans – you didn't then really, it was just about earning enough money to get by. And I suppose as a girl you weren't expected to have a career then anyway. That was left to the men.

Even if I had put more time and effort in at school, a job like a secretary or teacher or anything was out of the question. That would have been a career for more middle-class or rich girls, so pretty much all the girls round my way ended up working in one of the factories.

Hardly motivation to study, was it? And there were always so many jobs going in them that it wasn't like today when you had to fight for your job, it was easy to get one. And if you need any proof of that, just listen to this! On my first day of job hunting I headed out of my flat and went to the next street along from Watts Grove, called Violet Road. Them days it was filled with factories most all the way along, with a few houses dotted in between. The factories weren't big, like they were years later. They were more like converted buildings that could be right in the middle of a row of houses without anyone batting an eyelid. To get in, you normally went through what looked like a garage door, and the factory opened out behind.

Anyway, as I was walking along Violet Road, I saw an advert for a vacancy stuck on the door of a cork factory – I forget the name 'cause 'the cork factory' was all we ever used to call it – and I just knocked on the door and they were like 'come in', and they gave me the job almost as soon as I walked in. I think they literally asked where I lived and how old I was. You had to have proof by taking along what was officially called a 'certified copy of an entry of birth for the purposes of employment of young people' that the government gave you. The rest of us just knew it as a proof of age certificate. You had to get it signed to prove you were old enough to work. Anyway, once I showed that, they just asked when I could start. So I got the first job I tried for, and within minutes of me starting the search!

I started work the very next day, and spent the morning being trained in what to do, then by the afternoon I was considered capable of doing the job, and got on with it alongside the other workers.

The cork factory, like most factories then, didn't have any windows. So each morning the doors would swing open at the time you started work, everyone would head in, and they'd close behind you, and that would be you shut in for the day. Goodbye daylight and all that!

It was a long room with machinery either side and then there was a little room above at the end where the guv'nor would sit keeping an eye on you, suddenly hollering out things like 'Pat Spicer, come up here!' and all that business, when he wanted a word about rotas, pay, or what have you.

It was all very basic, apart from the machinery – I mean it was just concrete floors, no carpet or anything. All you had were these big speakers that we played the radio through, or records – that kept people in a happier mood than silence, definitely. You'd get more lost in your work like that.

My job was making corks that went in bottles, though you don't get them now like the ones that we made. It wasn't like the fat corks you get in wine bottles or whatever. They were the tiny little thin ones that went in bottles, like beer and all that.

And what was my job? Well, there were these huge sheets of cork and you had a big handle that stamped down on them, cutting through them to make the little corks, and that was all I had to do really, like printing them out. I did thousands a day. Problem was you were on piece work, which means you were paid according to how much work you did, not just the hours. So you had to get so many of the sheets out to get paid the maximum, which meant you always had to rush and be working at top speed if you wanted to get as much money as you could.

It weren't a bad job, though, and it only took me about five minutes to get there from my flat. You'd come out the building each morning, walk down the road, cut through a little alleyway and you were there.

But, oh, the guv'nor was a stickler for timekeeping. You had to clock in and clock out by taking your card from this kind of board that had all your names on it, stamp it and put it back. If you were one minute late in the morning you would lose a quarter of an hour's pay, and you daren't clock out a minute before your time, otherwise you'd lose a quarter of an hour then too. You'd always lose time somewhere along the way if they could help it.

But it was good, I enjoyed it, and there were some nice people working there. There were a few girls I would sit and talk with in my lunch break – you'd get half an hour, and we would go and sit outside on the garden walls of the houses roundabout and chat. I was one of the youngest, so mostly I'd sit and listen as the other girls talked about boyfriends and going out – they always seemed more mature and to be having more fun than I was. It made me a bit jealous and mad at my dad for not letting me out more. I liked hearing their stories, though.

You couldn't go far from your machines over lunch, you didn't have long enough. So it wasn't like I could go home for lunch. I'd bring in sandwiches with me each day. You had to supply your own food – just about all you could expect was to get paid by the boss, there was no way they'd give you a lunch too!

The factory was all women except for a few men who used to carry in the big sheets of cork. A van would arrive outside the door, and they'd bring the cork in for you.

Then each Friday you would go and get your money from the guv'nor. It would be in a brown envelope and what hours you had done and how much you had earned and all that business was written on it. You didn't pay national insurance or tax or anything then, so it was just cash. On a good week I would say I earned £2. But it would have been a very good week for that – most often I topped up my pay packet with what they called homework.

There used to be a lady in the factory who would come round at the end of every day with a pushchair full of sacks of these corks and these metal lids. The idea was the cork needed to be pushed into the lid to create a lid made of both parts. Imagine the old beer bottles with the metal lids – a bit like you get on flip-top caps of beer today. But then they had cork inside them too to make them seal tighter. Well, that's what you were fitting together. And that was all you had to do at home, separate to your day in the factory, if you agreed to it.

She'd offer you 10 bob – that's 10 shillings or 50p in today's money – if you could do a sack overnight. You had to have it done by the morning – and you needed that whole night to do it. You'd get home, have a bath and put on your nightdress and sit up all night doing the job by hand. Sometimes you'd cut yourself on the metal, but mostly it was pretty straightforward work. You just had to be fast at it. Then you would take the completed sack in the next day and she would come round and collect them.

If you were saving for something it was a good thing to do. Everyone was just very practical about it – you want the extra money, you put in the hours and earn it. And the best thing of all about it? It was the first time I actually had money that was mine. It's amazing how grown up and independent that can make you feel.

I was still living at home, and though I didn't pay rent, I used to give my dad a couple of bob out of my pay packet, just for living expenses really – towards the food shopping, which of course I was still in charge of, as well as the cleaning. I quickly learned to adapt my jobs around the working day. Nipping to the shop straight from work, getting up early to do the washing, whatever worked best around it all.

But other than my contribution to housekeeping, my wages was my money to buy my own stuff as I wanted. So I'd use it to get my own clothes for the first time. I remember the first pair of shoes I bought myself. They were these wedges that were fashionable then. It was the first time I had been able to see something I liked and decide to go for it. And the first time I had been able to react to a fashion!

Because fashion still existed even then, of course. It was just whether you could afford to follow it was a different matter. And it didn't come in and out so quickly – a fashion probably lasted a year or two, rather than a season, going in and out before you know it like nowadays.

I also remember full gathered skirts being quite a fashion, like they have been again recently. Where you had layers of net petticoats underneath and an elasticated waist. We'd get one of those and wear it with a nice flimsy blouse.

What I didn't really use my money on was going out. I never really went out – because my dad wouldn't let me. As I said, after my mum died, he became quite a domineering man, my dad. It was always 'you can't do this' and 'you can't do that' sort of business. I'm sure he meant well and was being more overprotective than anything, but it was still frustrating.

There were three places really that I was allowed to go, and I went to each of them once a week if I could.

The first was the pictures. I'd go to the Hippodrome in Poplar with Win, or one of my cousins, but it's not there any more. It was just a shilling to get in, but if you were feeling flush, you'd go to the Odeon at Mile End. That was a big one facing the station, and it was very expensive – half a crown to get in there. I remember that a lot of the stars used to go there when a big film came out, I guess for the premieres.

I went to the first showing of *The Black Rose*, a film about a couple of lads who head off on an adventure to

China. Tyrone Power starred in it if I remember right. Oh, Tyrone Power . . . he was a real star, and stunning! The evening sticks in my mind less for the film, though, and more 'cause they gave every single person who was there a black rose. I thought that was really clever, and I took mine home and tried to dry it and keep it afterwards.

But more memorable than that at the Odeon was an appearance by Omar Sharif for a film of his that was being released. Oh, I'll never forget that! I'd gone with one of my cousins and we got so excited. We had to walk the mile or so up there because we couldn't afford the bus fare at that time. But all the way there we were giddy with excitement, and we got there just as he was going in. He was only a young man at the time, but I remember him as this great big tall fellow with a moustache and looking ever so elegant. We thought he was so lovely. We discussed that night non-stop for ages after, and I properly dreamed about him for quite some time! That night really sticks in my mind. It is probably one of my favourite memories from those years.

He was the only celebrity I saw really, until *The Only Way Is Essex* began and I started going to events all the celebrities were at. Then I started seeing them a lot. But back then, well, that was the only time, as far as I remember, that I ever saw anyone famous.

In them days, though, there wasn't the same thing with celebrities that there is today. People didn't have the same total worship of someone just 'cause they were famous. It was only actors that got to being well known 'cause of seeing them at the cinema. But they were so far removed from our own lives, that it never seemed like your paths would actually cross. They were just someone that you kind of knew of from films. It was hard to even imagine that they were real people! I would never have had posters up on my wall of stars or anything like that.

There were newspapers then of course, but they didn't write about celebrities in that way. It was more things about the war, or crime or politics. I remember the *Mirror* being a popular one in my area, though I don't think the *Sun* existed at that time. Not that we had any of them in our house – we never had any books or newspapers, least not to read, only for toilet paper! I'm certain I never saw my parents read, but I don't know if they just didn't enjoy books or newspapers, if there wasn't the time 'cause there was too much else to do, or more likely, 'cause they couldn't read. It was a lot more normal in them days that people couldn't read – it is not like today's obsession with getting every child good at reading and maths and the like.

Either way, I never read a newspaper, and we didn't

even have television at that time, so people didn't know celebrities that way. It was only just before I left home that I remember my dad got his first television set. A tiny little thing that you could hardly see anything on. It was a good few years before they started getting bigger.

Anyhow, as well as the cinema, I also went over to the church once a week for a kind of social thing, I guess it was like a youth club. We just sat around and had a little chat to one another, and a sing-song if they had any good records on. It was all the singers of the time, such as Vera Lynn, Doris Day and Frankie Laine.

I would never have bought a record in those days, but my favourite singers were the Beverley Sisters. They were these three girls from Bethnal Green, twins called Teddie and Babs, and their older sister Joy, who always used to stand in the middle. I remember them being all blonde and stylish, and doing these great songs that I could listen to over and over again.

At this club at the church, they had an old gramophone that they'd wind up and we'd listen to for a while, but otherwise, that was it, then we'd go home! I suppose like now, some girls would meet boys at youth clubs, but then I was so shy it was never going to come to anything. You'd sort of look at someone and all that business and then you'd get all frightened and come away and that was it. Although, tell a lie, I did have my first kiss at this youth club with a fella whose name I have forgotten. I had noticed him a few times, silly glances like, and then he came over to talk to me – there was no way I'd make the first move! And I ended up having a couple of kisses with him as we were leaving at the end of an evening, but they weren't like proper snog kisses, just silly little ones, and then I ran away! I don't think I can really count that as a first kiss, can I? It makes me blush even thinking about it now!

There were other churches in the area too that ran social evenings that we'd go to sometimes for a change. I forget the names of the churches, but it was just a different way to add some variety to your evenings.

But out of the things I was allowed to do, forget the cinema and church social meetings, my favourite was when once a week me and Winnie used to go speedway riding. Not like actually do it, of course, but to watch it. It was on motorbikes, going around this track in Westham somewhere. I'm surprised my dad let me go really – although thinking about it, maybe he didn't realize where I was off to!

You would pay tenpence to get in – pence, not 'p', as in those days if you wanted to shorten it down it was to 'd' – then you'd stand out in the open and watch them go round the track, but you never wanted to get too close because God help you if one of the pebbles on the track flew up and got you in the eye or whatever. They got up some speed. And then you'd say to each other 'he'll win' or 'that one'll win'. It was like placing bets, but we never used to actually pay or anything. Looking back I enjoyed that, I rightly did.

Anyway, after about a year or eighteen months at the cork factory, I had had enough of working there, and decided to change to a different job. So I had a bit of a look around to see what other places were looking for workers, and found a job in a knicker factory on Bow Road. I decided that would be more fun, and I didn't mind sewing, so I got a job there, and handed my one week's notice in at the cork factory.

The knicker place was in an old garage-type building again, as they all were then, and was exactly opposite that church that sits in the middle of the road, St Mary and Holy Trinity church. I can never quite believe it is still there, with a main road running either side of it! But it seems to survive, so good on it.

But anyway, back then there was just the one road, on one side of it, and our factory was on the other. It had a little green garage-like door, and you went through, and it opened out into a bigger room that was our work area, filled with machines. You never had big factories in them days, I don't think they were allowed.

So in there we were making silk knickers, proper pure, quality silk knickers. And camisole tops too, although not bras. The best thing was where the material came from – it was from the barrage balloons from the war! Remember the balloons I described earlier that used to float over the city? Well, when the war ended, they had no more use for them, so they got them down and cut them all up into strips of material, and that is where we came in. We'd be sat there with our electric machines that you operated with a foot pedal, stitching away, making these old balloons into lovely new underwear.

Most of the balloons were grey coloured, although there were some kind of dark cream ones too. And obviously we didn't want to just make grey or cream underwear. So some of the material must have been dyed in a machine further down the factory 'cause I remember stitching underwear of all sorts of colours.

The fashion in knickers then was for camiknickers. They were elasticated at the waist and underneath you would have three buttons so you could go to the toilet without having to take the whole thing down. Or sometimes you had knickers with the button at the side. They were a loose, short type of style, so that they would still go over the top of your suspender belt without looking odd, although tighter styles were starting to come about as I was leaving the factory, if I remember.

We would all sit there in these long rows, like a big production line, behind these huge sewing machines. And everyone had their set job.

You never done a whole piece of clothing, everyone had a small job within the process to do before passing it on. So it would start with the girls down one end who were cutting up the material, according to set patterns, then it would get passed along for people to sew different bits, and I was one of them. It was my job to stitch the sides of these camiknickers. Then someone else would do the round bits, someone else would put the buttons on, it was like that. So in a day, I did a bit towards dozens of pairs of underwear. As with the cork factory, I had been given just a half-day's training at the start, but it was straightforward enough work.

A foreman, or mostly a forelady, would keep an eye on things, and make sure you were doing a good job. Occasionally you made a mistake, but not often – as with elsewhere, we were paid by piece, rather than an hourly rate, so you did your best to keep going right. Unpicking any mistakes was timely and costly.

It was a fun place to work. And I remember there were a lot of jokes and chat going on, in amongst all the speedy stitchwork! Looking back, I can't remember why I left there as it was good fun.

The next place I went was Yardley's, a perfume

factory in Stratford. You took on a different role in the factory each week, but mostly it was bottling the perfume up, putting labels on, or putting little rubber stoppers into the top of the bottles. Then later they swapped the stoppers for little screw-top lids. It was lavender and all that sort of thing. Or I say all that sort of thing, but really it was all just lavender. That was pretty much the only smell you could get in a perfume them days. None of all these fancy thousands of different smells, and perfumes named after celebrities, and all that. You smelled of lavender, or you just smelt! Lavender perfume, lavender water, or lavender bags that you would put in your knicker drawer or hang up around the place so that your room smelt nice.

And there was no getting away from your job at the end of the day, for you'd take the smell with you. When you got on the bus, what was it, six o'clock every night, all the folks on there would go, 'Ooh, they have all come from Yardley's. Smell 'em!' and everyone would smell you, as all the workers made the whole bus smell nice of lavender.

But sadly, much as I enjoyed the job, I was only there a couple of months before I had to leave – or, if I'm gonna be honest, I got the sack – for pinching the perfume! The bleedin' things I have been up to . . .

Oh, honestly, it was bad. But I remember everyone

used to say, 'Wrap up that bottle and put it in your knickers or in your bra' or, 'Get that lavender bag and put it in your turban'. And everyone was at it – a bit like all the factories really. It was sort of seen as fair game to take a little bit of what you were dealing with. Then when you got on the bus, all the women would whip out what they had taken and swap it to their handbags. And sometimes I kept it for myself, and sometimes I sold it on to other people.

Anyway, somehow they must have found out we were doing it 'cause me and my friend were hauled in front of the guv'nor. And he said, 'We understand that you are both stealing perfumes.'

I was rightly terrified, and just kept quiet and shook my head, only speaking to deny it. But my friend piped up, 'What do we want this muck for, like? No chance we've been stealing it!'

That was it then, that made him mad, and we were ordered to take our turbans off, and, of course, the bottles just fell to the floor, didn't they? So we got the sack straightaway. I was so annoyed because everyone was at it, and we were the ones who got bleedin' caught!

Especially 'cause my mum had been doing it all those years and getting away with it. I was letting the side down. And I never did find out why the bosses particularly targeted us . . .

Then I went to a sack place down by Bromley-by-Bow and oh, that was an awful job. Basically we were cleaning out these cloth sacks that would come in all dirty and rotten. Anything might have been in them – potatoes, coal . . . they might have come from farms, or everywhere and anywhere. I mean I'll be honest, we did just used to call it 'shit'. 'We've got to clean the shit out of these bags', mostly 'cause you didn't actually know what it was that had been in them.

So you'd have these great big barrels filled with sacks, and you'd have five or six girls round you. Then you'd get hold of the sacks and turn them inside out, and shake them. Then you'd hold them in front of what they called a big blower, like this big industrial air blower, that would blow all the rubbish out.

You'd be holding on tight 'cause you didn't dare let go and be the one to disrupt the work flow, and it would blow it clean.

Then you would put the clean sack into another barrel and it would be taken away to be filled up again with whatever stuff was needed.

Oh, it was awful, horrible, dirty work. You would get covered in dust and whatever else was in the sack, and go home stinking. It suddenly made getting on the bus smelling awful strong of lavender seem like a good thing. I only stuck it out for a couple of months because, honest to God, it was an absolute hell hole.

You got through a lot of those days with chat and laughter and jokes. There was a real atmosphere in some of these factories 'cause having fun with each other was the best way through it. There was a very dry East End humour running through it all as well, jokes that probably outsiders wouldn't have understood. But everyone dealt with life by using it.

I developed a line that I used quite a lot at that time when I got annoyed with people commenting on my small height – I'm only five foot.

'Ain't you little?' they'd always say.

And I'd reply, 'Yeah, well, when I started this job I was six foot tall and thirty stone.'

'Was you really?' some of them would reply.

Oh, wake up, please! If they couldn't have a laugh about something like that, or weren't switched on enough to realize . . . well, it was a good way for me to work out which were the ones I wanted to be friends with, and who were the fools I wanted to avoid . . .

By this time, although I was getting older – I was about seventeen, my dad was as strict as ever on me going out. So while I saw some of my friends off courting, and a couple of girls in the area were even starting to get married, there was no way I could get involved with boys. So I was forever having to find ways to enjoy myself that didn't annoy him at the same time – it was just easier to avoid a row when I could. Which is one reason I did enjoy our street party for the Queen's Coronation. It was a party, but held on the courtyard in front of our flats, so there was no way he could object.

I vaguely remember Elizabeth's father King George VI dying the year before, but more because it was a talking point around our dinner table and amongst neighbours for some time. I don't remember his actual funeral.

The party for Elizabeth becoming queen was on 2 June 1953. It was a Tuesday, but it was a national holiday so everyone was off. We had trestle tables laid out in our courtyard area and everyone brought some food. There wasn't any alcohol that I remember – or tiddly as I called it – or if there was, that was just for the men. The women would have been drinking tea and lemonade. We made big jugs of it. The proper stuff mind, not like today, full of chemicals. This stuff was made from lemonade crystals, which you'd buy in a tin, then you added water, and got the real good proper-tasting drink. Everyone crowded around the radio when it was time for the coronation – no one had a television – so we just listened to it on the wireless. Then after the food there was music played through a gramophone and all the adults and the kids had a dance to it.

Everyone had to wear red, white and blue, and one lady made matching pinafores for all the girls. It must have taken her weeks. We hung little flags and banners on string from one balcony landing to the next across the gardens – oh, a lot of preparation went into that party! It was a real community event. Everyone in all the blocks around joined in – and nearby buildings had their own parties. I remember someone gathered everyone together for an official group photograph, and we all got a copy of it a couple of weeks later. It's in black and white and I am up at the back, looking a bit shy – I wasn't that keen on having my photo taken. But it's a great memento of the day.

In them days everyone was a royalist. I think the royal family is a good thing, and the Queen's done so well, especially where she is today at her age. She really is a grand old lady. Her mum was the same, the old Queen Mum. She liked a drop of tiddly, didn't she?! Good luck to her, she had nothing to lose. And she was so tiny, but so feisty, you could see it in her.

I've never seen any of the royal family in person, even though they have done visits around the East End. And, do you know, I hadn't even visited Buckingham Palace until earlier this year. I knew where it was, like, but even though I've been a Londoner all my life I'd never ever been. Terrible innit! But that's how it was.

You didn't have time for those things. Being a tourist and doing visits and that was for rich people. And anyway, although it was London, it wasn't my bit of London. We hardly ever left the Devons Road and Bow area for anything.

All the same, whether we had met her or not, having a party was our way of telling the Queen 'well done' from us.

THIRTEEN
My Charlie

The first time I set eyes on my husband Charlie was the autumn of 1953 and I was seventeen, nearly eighteen. And I can't say I knew I was going to marry him straightaway or anything, but I knew I'd have liked to!

Like I said, the flats in Bilberry House were owned by the council – as they pretty much all were in our whole area – and at the time the heating came from the coal fires. Finally the council had decided to take them out and put in boilers for heating instead – for safety reasons and generally modernizing, I suppose. And it just so happened that, as fate would have it, a young man called Charlie Brooker worked for the council at that time. One day he came knocking round Bilberry House as part of this boiler installation, and told my dad, 'We gotta come in and take your fireplace out.'

Well, I wasn't home at the time, but my dad being

a decorator, he'd just done the place up, and that evening he told me about the visit.

'Make sure they don't make this place a mess. That's all I've got to say,' he said, sounding annoyed.

'Alright, alright,' I said, knowing I'd have to take a day off work to keep an eye while these council workers did what they had to.

Well, this fella Charlie turns up the next morning to do the work, and I got all shy, didn't I, for he was right dashing and really lovely. He was a big tall strong fella with thick dark hair and sparkly kind eyes and a certain way about him. I know it sounds daft, but he really was the man of my dreams – forget Omar Sharif!

But it was only me who was shy out of the two of us – he wasn't shy in the slightest. Not Charlie! He was as cheeky as they come and started to talk almost as soon as he was through the door. You know, almost one of his first questions was, 'Courting, love?'! I shook my head. 'Not got a fella, a pretty girl like you? Shame on the lads round here!'

He started work in our front room, and I just stood there in the corner with my head down, too frightened to talk, and trying not to look at him. Seeing he wasn't getting an answer, he soon followed it up with, 'Gonna make a cup of tea, girl?' and I scurried out and did it, relieved at the excuse to escape along with my blushes.

Then the next day he came back to carry on the work, and it was the same kind of chat. Then bold as brass, he went, 'Can I take you out?' as straightforward as that! I didn't know what to say, and mumbled, 'Yeah, yeah, alright, yeah.' But we never did set any proper arrangements up. I think he sensed I was too shy at that stage, and I wouldn't have dared as my dad would never have allowed me.

But this routine of flirtation and pretence at dates went on for weeks, 'cause they were working their way around all the flats in our building, so he was always at one or another of them. And I secretly knew I liked him, but was too shy to speak to him, so I'd stand out on the balcony and just watch where he was at each day. Whenever he saw me he'd ask me out again, or say 'alright, see you tonight', all cocky as can be, and I'd always just nod and say 'alright' 'cause I didn't know what else to say. We never got as far as arranging a meeting place, so I knew he was just teasing me, or, I suppose, flirting! Testing out the water, like.

Then one night there was a knock at the door, and my dad went out to answer it and Charlie was standing there. I can remember their conversation as clear as day. It went like this:

'Yeah?', my dad growled.

'Oh, is Pat there?'

'Why, what do you want?'

'Well, I'm the fellow that was doing your fireplace . . .'

'Oh, are you! Well, come in here a minute. I'll tell you what, come in, have you seen the state . . .'

And he hollered and hooted at him, and really gave him what for. I don't suppose the front room had really been left in a state by normal standards, but 'cause like I said, it was my dad's job, he was quite a perfectionist about it. And after he'd got that out of his system a bit, with Charlie just standing listening, then the conversation went on:

'So what is it you've come round for?'

'To take Pat out.'

'Oh, have you? She's not going out with you or anybody else, so sling your hook!'

And that was it, Charlie was out the door. Oh, I was ashamed, weren't I? He knew how to make me feel bad, my dad. I knew he wouldn't let me go. I never went outside the door if he could help it, except for work and church. But I suppose there was a bit inside me that had really hoped this would be the first time he would have relented. It wasn't to be.

Anyhow, the next day, I saw Charlie in the flats and went to apologize.

'Oh, don't worry,' he said. 'I'll send someone round

to sort your dad's place if he's not happy with the job we done.'

'You better not,' I said. 'He does it all himself.'

And that was like the ice breaker, then we started to talk more, like actual conversations. Not that I let my dad know I was meeting Charlie for chats. He never would have allowed it.

I didn't lie to my dad, I just used to do it behind his back without him knowing. I'd say, 'I'm just going out for a little while, I won't be long', and then I used to meet Charlie downstairs. We used to go round the corner and there were these old-fashioned baths that you could use to do your washing and all that business. Not like swimming baths, but proper actual baths. It was like a building full of baths which you could go and use 'cause lots of people didn't actually have them in those days. Or some people would go and do their washing there too 'cause again washing machines didn't exist.

Or you could go if you had something wrong with you, like nits in your hair, or fleas, or what they called scabies. You went in there and they would hose you down and put this stuff all over you. You'd especially see people in there that were particularly dirty for whatever reason, or who had been living rough. Not that any of this was of interest to us, we were all about each other! It just happened that the corner by this place was a good place to stand and talk.

That happened for a couple of months, just innocent conversation, getting to know each other. I learned that Charlie was born in 1930, so he was five and a half years older than me and was twenty-three at that time. Explains why he always seemed more worldly wise I suppose, 'cause he was!

The actual date he was born was 13 April, which he always joked was an unlucky day for the world, but not for me! Charlie being born was my lucky day indeed. He was from a proper working-class background like mine, but he lived over in Canning Town which was a couple of miles away from Devons Road.

Then one day he asked me to go to the pictures, and I said yes, which in them days meant we were courting. As soon as a boy asked you to go out in the evening – and really pictures was the only thing you ever went to – you were officially courting.

Why is it no one knows what courting means now? Now it's all, 'I'm going out with so and so.' Then you talked about people courting – it was the same thing really, just another word for dating.

We used to go to the picture palace a lot up on Chrisp Street, although it is not there any more. But you know, I can't remember any of the films we saw 'cause we were always sitting at the back, and kissing and cuddling! To be honest I suppose that was the main reason a lot of couples went to the pictures. It was the one place you could be together in the dark, with people not worrying that it was inappropriate.

Afterwards we would walk back hand in hand and do our little bit of courting by those old baths, and stand there 'til it was time that I had to go back up. My dad always set me a curfew. It was 9 or 10 p.m., depending on his mood that day.

As far as what you wore on a date, well, you didn't have much choice of clothes, so it was maybe a case of just putting on a clean top. People didn't pay the same attention to new clothing then as now. And I wasn't really interested in make-up, other than lipstick.

My dad would never let me wear make-up. He used to say, 'I hope you don't put all that muck on your face' and I'd go, 'No, I don't use nothing like that.' But unbeknown to him, as soon as I came out the flat and went down the stairs, I'd get my lipstick out of my pocket or bag and put it on. Only a little, and that was the only bit of make-up I did wear, but it was a thing I started doing for Charlie.

Charlie had an older brother and sister called Dickie and Mary, and a younger half-sister, also called Pat – or Patti as she was known. I got on well with them all, but

I remember that Mary always used to have lots of make-up, and I used to be quite in awe of it, but when she tried to get me to put any on, I'd say I didn't want to try it. Or I say a lot of make-up, but not compared with these days. I just mean as well as lippy she would have had some powder, and maybe a little something for her eyes.

It was only after I got married that I started wearing a bit more make-up. But I've never been big on it really – none of this whole Essex look with the fake eyelashes and tan for me, thank you very much. I'll leave that to the grandkids.

Me and Winnie were still friends at this point, but I'll tell you what, we nearly had a falling out over Charlie! He told me one time, 'I could have took Winnie out. She was after me.'

'What?!' I snapped, outraged. 'Yeah,' he kept teasing. 'She was making eyes at me and making it very clear she was after me!' I was furious. But then I decided I couldn't blame her for being interested in him – after all he was a great catch!

By then I think my dad had begun to realize what was happening between the two of us – he'd probably suspected since the first night Charlie called at the flat, and I'm sure gossip made its way back to him – so he did what he could to stop it. He'd make sure I had an early curfew on nights he suspected I was seeing Charlie. And when it finally became too obvious to ignore when Charlie called at the flat for me, my dad argued with Charlie for a while, but when Charlie stood his ground and said we had arrangements, he backed down and just gave us a curfew of 10 p.m. But while he accepted we were courting, he still made it very difficult, and clear that Charlie wasn't welcome – he would never let Charlie into the flat, or encourage me to go and see him. He'd always say to me, 'It won't last, you don't want to go courting.' Or his favourite line was, 'He's never going to stick by you.'

Oh, he was forever coming out with this, that and the other, you know, anything that might plant a negative idea in my mind. But it didn't work. I knew what I thought of Charlie by this time, that he was a good man, and that I was in love with him. Besides, I had inherited a stubborn streak off my dad, which up until now I had kept hidden, out of respect for him. I hadn't always agreed with what he'd said, but I'd obeyed it. But this was the one area of my life I wasn't willing to budge on.

Anyhow, I remember one night when Charlie couldn't get home back to his in Canning Town because it was thick fog, absolute total thick fog. He used to get to mine by bus, or sometimes by walking, which would have taken about an hour.

Anyhow, that night, there was gonna be no buses running, and it was going to be an awful walk home, unable to see your hand in front of your face.

'Can he stay, Dad?' I begged.

'No, he can't. You let him find his own way home,' Dad said straightaway.

Oh, that was harsh that was, but he stuck to it, and true enough, poor Charlie did have to go. I'm sure nights like that he must have wondered if it was worth courting me, when he had my dad to deal with too.

Then another time, a couple of months later, we found ourselves in a similar predicament, but this time it was snowing, and really badly. And I asked the same thing.

'Can't he stay, Dad? He really can't get home,' I said.

'I don't care,' Dad said.

I was so upset, but at the finish, after I'd whimpered and pleaded a bit more, he let him stay. Charlie was so grateful. 'I'll stay on the settee,' he offered straightaway.

'No, you won't. You'll get in my bed,' Dad replied, just as quick. Now poor Charlie thought this meant my dad was having a sudden turn of kindness, and that Dad was giving up his bed for him, so we went, 'Oh no, I don't wanna . . .'

'Oh, you're not pushing me out,' Dad said grimly. 'I'll sleep one end, you sleep the other end.'

And I swear to God, they spent the night fully clothed in the same bed, each with one eye open. If my Charlie was still here, even up to this day he'd tell you how clear that night was in his memory. He told me, 'I was dying to go to the toilet and I didn't dare get up because your father was lying there looking at me as much as to say, "You dare move, I'll kill ya".' I tell you, it's funny now, but at the time it was awful.

I don't know if my dad really thought Charlie would come sneaking into my bedroom or what, but he never would have. You could never have done that – you did nothing like that in front of your parents. You couldn't even kiss in front of them. I mean if we did want to kiss, we used to walk out into the alleyway, and have a quick kiss on the lips, and then he'd go.

In fact, if you need proof of just how innocent I was, this little tale should do it – though I'm quite embarrassed to tell it!

Shortly after me and Charlie started courting, I got myself in quite a worry that I might be pregnant. Oh, I was terrified – can you imagine what would have happened? I hadn't been with Charlie long enough by then to be sure he'd have stayed with me and married me, and my dad . . . well. I don't know what he'd have done. I had myself convinced he'd kick me out anyhow.

So I got Winnie to come round my flat, and all quiet like, I went, 'I think I'm going to have a baby.'

'I'm gonna get my sister,' she said straightaway. And she raced upstairs for her sister Gracie, who I told you about before, who was a bit older than us, and the oldest Armitage daughter.

Gracie come down and went, 'What actually happened?'

I went all red with embarrassment, and with my head down, eventually I said, 'He kissed me and he touched my bum.'

'Yeah, what else?'

This floored me. 'Nothing else, that's it, that's all he done.'

'You're not going to get pregnant like that,' she laughed. 'You're not gonna have a baby.'

'I will! I'm gonna have a baby!'

'No you will not, not unless . . .'

And then she told me what things were all about, and how you actually had sex, and what to expect from it.

I was horrified, and went, 'Oh my God, oh no, please don't!' It sounded awful!

But she added – and she was very sure about this – 'Don't never let him do that unless you are married.'

At that stage, having heard about it all for the first time, I didn't think I'd ever let a man do that to me, married or not!

Thank goodness for Gracie, though – she sat down to tell me and Winnie everything about what was going to go on. I really had been properly clueless, and now I was petrified!

But really, how stupid can you get that I thought a kiss would get me pregnant? I was eighteen and didn't know the ways of the world at all. Today most kids half that age would know more than I did then.

But, then again, I never had anyone to tell me anything different, without my mum or an older sister, and they didn't teach you any of that stuff in school them days. The only ideas I had, I'd got off my nan, and, well . . . they only made me more confused with her strange sayings. She told me, 'Don't ever kiss any boys because you never know what's going to happen', so it's no wonder I had thought I was pregnant! She was always like, 'Don't do this with boys, don't do that . . .'

But I can't judge her for saying those things to me – more than likely her mum and nan had said exactly the same to her, if not to an even bigger extreme. But God forbid if she were alive now to know what actually does go on with half the kids today. Sleeping with one another before getting married, having babies first then getting married after, if at all . . . and she thought kissing a boy was so bad!

Meanwhile, life with Charlie kept getting better. We had a similar humour and outlook on life. And I looked up to him and really just saw him as a bit of a hero.

He was much more knowledgeable about life than me – but I have to say, not always in a way that I liked. Before his job in the council – what we called the London County Council, or LCC in them days – he had been in the Army, and then the Navy. And let's just say he knew what was what. He had been abroad, and he always used to tell me, 'I had a girl in Australia, and another in New Zealand, and here and there . . .'

Before that, when I'd heard what they say about sailors, that 'they have got one in every port', I didn't realize what they were talking about, and Charlie would laugh. If I asked him straight, though, 'Have you had another girl?' he'd say, 'Of course I haven't', but then he'd be back to talking about it, and I knew he had really.

I used to talk to Winnie about it. But I suppose we decided that's just the way it was – and in them days it was. Men could do what they wanted when they were single and girls couldn't. Sometimes I think it's the same today in a way really.

Anyway, after he left the Navy, he did one or two

other little jobs in different places, as you did then, before starting to work for the council.

He was also really into boxing, although he was giving it up around the time I met him. He was good and used to get quite a few medals and cups and trophies, but one day he just said, 'I'm not going to do it no more.' I don't know why, I think he just got the idea in his head that he was getting older, and he'd had his fun doing it, but he didn't want to no more.

Around this time I met a lady through Charlie, who was to become one of my favourite aunties of all time. She was called Alice – see, I know she was an especially close auntie 'cause I even know her name!

Her husband was Charlie's boss at the council, and I was fascinated by her. She was really over the top and flashy, and always had these big fur collars and animal wraps, still with the head on it, like a fox. It would be draped over her shoulders with this whole head on one end, looking at you like, and the tail still on the other. She loved those furs – even going out to get two pounds of potatoes, that fur would be around her shoulders. And she was so lovely and kind and friendly, and always had gossip and stories to tell. For whatever reason she took me under her wing, and from then onwards was always calling round to my home to see how I was doing. I think she quite liked mothering me if I'm honest.

One thing I loved doing with Charlie at this time was having a day out at the beach. We used to go to Southend for the day in the summer if it was nice and sunny. Everyone went to Southend at that time, either for the day or for holidays. It is on the coast in Essex and has miles of beaches. There was also a huge long pleasure pier that stretched more than a mile out to sea that would be filled with crowds of people. It had a really good atmosphere with everyone just having fun.

Going there was about the only time I ever got the train, and it was still the old-fashioned steam ones where the carriages had small compartments, so you could be quite private. It felt very posh and mature to be getting the train and having an area to ourselves.

One thing I didn't do, though, was swim in the sea. I'm petrified of water. Don't get me wrong, I love showering and bathing, I'm a very clean person, not a dirty one! But I'm always frightened the water's going to cover my eyes, I fear that I'm going to drown. I'll mostly try anything else, I've got good guts for other things, but swimming, ugh, no. So the most I would do is paddle in the sea, and I've sat down in it near the edge, but I don't like it going past my stomach. If it starts to cover me over I'll panic. It's terrible isn't it, but that was how I was!

Besides, them days they didn't teach you to swim at

school, so I had never learned. I suppose if you learn as a child you just accept it, but once you are older and you know you can drown, your mind doesn't let you.

The other way I went to Southend a couple of times was on these outings called beanos. Up until now, I hadn't gone on them. It was my dad who had been a big fan of going there on beanos. What they were was basically a day out for the men and their friends to have fun and get tiddly. They would set off early in the morning on a coach, taking crates of beer with them and a lunch of sandwiches, boiled eggs and tomatoes. Then they would head to Southend, which really is only just up the road, but they would go to all sorts of different places along the way, and stop for a drink each time. I remember the Halfway House at Basildon was a very popular stopping-point. So by the time they reached Southend, they were well on their way to being merry.

Then once there they would go in the Kursaal, a big amusement hall, the first in the world apparently! It's only come down recently, but it was this big dome building that everyone knew, with a circus and casino and ballroom inside. There was a big fair there too with a big wheel, a water shoot, bumper cars, and the lady who tells your fortune.

And Southend would be full of other people all on

beanos, so they'd all meet up and have fun. Women too – women went on beanos as well, but you never set out on the same day. You went separately. It was either the men's turn or the women's. My dad loved those days out.

It was the local pub that would organize them, with the landlord advertising a month or so ahead that it was happening, to give people a chance to put their names down and pay in instalments. People would hand over a bob or two a week from their pay packet so that it didn't seem so costly, then that would be their travel and beers organized.

Soon after I met Charlie I found out he was a fan of them too, and he would head off for a day with the boys, so I got curious and decided I'd try them out. I went a few times and they were good fun. All the girls together, singing and joking on the bus, and then you had a good day out when you got to Southend, but I'm not sure it was worth it when I got home. No, these beanos were what caused some of mine and Charlie's first rows, 'cause he was not happy with me going on them.

'Who you been kissing today?' he'd ask as soon as I got back.

'No one!'

'Likely story, come on tell me!'

Oh, it was the one thing that really got him going all jealous, so much so that it was hardly worth going on them, so annoying was he when I got back! Oh dear.

FOURTEEN

The Big Day

After two years, Charlie proposed. It wasn't like a romantic proposal, I don't actually even remember where it happened, but it was more just a conversation about the practical side of things.

'Let's get married,' he said one day. 'It's about time we got married.'

'Yeah, alright,' I said, and that was it. But I was secretly grinning inside. I'd known it was going to happen – them days you didn't court for two years unless marriage was what you were going to do at the end of it. But it was still a good feeling to hear it.

We started making plans, but there was one big problem in the way – Dad. I knew I couldn't come straight out and tell him my plans. I kept hinting at it to try and warm him up to the idea, but it was never met with a good response.

'Charlie's been really good to me. I think he'd make a good husband.'

'Well, you better think again, girl, 'cause it's not happening.'

'But Dad . . .'

'Forget it. I'm not discussing it.'

But at the same time, we were also disagreeing over another relationship, only this time it was his. For a while I had suspected he was having a bit of a thing with a woman who lived near us in our block of flats. I'd had a feeling all the way along 'cause there always seemed to be some excuse for him to be at her flat or the other way around, although he never admitted it for a long time. But eventually he came clean. Well, sure enough that decided it for me – why shouldn't I be planning to get married when he was moving on from Mum? It was seven years on now, but it didn't make it easy for me to think of him with another woman. I still missed her like crazy, of course I did. You couldn't help but think about her, especially at family times like Christmas or birthdays. But that is life I suppose.

The woman was called Bet Abrahams, and she had a husband already, but he was in a mental hospital. I wouldn't say I didn't like her, but I wasn't exactly friendly towards her. I felt like she tried to get favour with me by giving me money, or trying to be friendly. And then buying favour with my dad by backing him up about Charlie and telling me, 'You don't want to get married'. Little did she know by saying that she gave me, as a stubborn teen, the final push I needed to decide that walking down the aisle with my Charlie would definitely be the right thing!

She had children of her own too, two boys and two girls, all older than me. But at the time I thought they were too false for me. I was used to straight talking, not putting on niceties. We went out with them as a family a few times, and they used to come and put their arms around me and be like 'my sister Pat', as if they were trying to make themselves have love for me that they didn't really have. I don't think I could put my finger on it, but I just thought, 'I'm not your sister, why are you doing that?' I felt they were using me or trying to take me over, and I wouldn't have it.

Someone has said to me since then that I was being selfish, and perhaps I was. Or maybe in the same way that my dad didn't want to let me go 'cause it had just been the two of us for so long, I didn't actually want to let him go and move on to new people. It was a strange situation, and I feel terrible when I think about it now, but I just know back then it didn't make me happy to see him getting together with her.

It didn't help that I didn't really feel like I had a close

friend to talk things through with any more neither. Winnie and I had drifted apart. Once we were both working we didn't see as much of each other, and once I met Charlie that meant I had even less spare time.

Then she met an American man – I don't know how, and I never met him myself – but she got married around this time and they moved to America. That basically meant a complete end to things for me and Winnie, because our only means of contact would have been writing, and neither of us were bothered with letters. Besides, she was a newlywed, so her mind would have been elsewhere!

But I did miss having her to talk to about things and thought it was a shame we had grown apart. It would have been nice to have had a girl's take on everything that was going on in my life at that time. I have wondered since what has happened to her, but I don't suppose I'll ever know. Strange to have someone who was so important at one point in your life, then completely leave it. No mother, no sister, and no best friend. It wasn't good!

At least I had my Charlie. The problem was, the better things went with Charlie, the worse things went with my dad, until finally they came to a head. I suppose it was the inevitable thing that was going to happen.

When it had just been about me, and me not being

allowed out, or having to do all the housework, I could deal with that. I didn't know much better really. But when it affected things with Charlie, that was a different matter. I saw my future with him, and felt very strongly about spending time with him. So there were a lot of clashes in our house over those two years that we were courting, but more than ever when my dad realized how serious it was getting.

Not that I would argue too strongly – in them days you ultimately respected what your parents said, and backed down long before you would these days, even on things where you felt strongly. But even when I didn't show it, inside me I was not budging from my opinion.

One night we were arguing. It was just before Christmas, and I was nineteen by this time. I think it was the same old thing, where I was about to go and meet Charlie, and my dad was criticizing and trying to stop me. I took it a step further and tested the water.

'Dad, I won't be coming home tonight,' I said. I didn't have a definite plan in mind, but I think I just wanted to push my limits and see what happened. But it turned out that was a step beyond what my dad thought was acceptable.

'Well, do that and you can stay out all the time,' he snapped. 'Pack your bags and get out, my girl!'

And because my dad wasn't the only person in the

house with a stubborn streak in him, I got a fit in my head. Although I am sure he didn't mean it, I chose to take him at his word, packed up a bag, and left.

Charlie was already waiting outside and he just took me straight over to his. I'd already told his mum what it was like over at my house, so I don't think she was surprised. She had probably seen it coming to be honest. She just said to me, 'It's no trouble, move in here and don't worry about it.'

So that was it. I moved in with Charlie and his mum in their family home at 5 Bray Drive in Canning Town, where Charlie had been born and lived all his life.

It was strange at first as I had only ever lived in the one place before, other than when I was evacuated, and my dad had always been around. But I was like part of their family for that time. I got on fine with his mum, and it was good for me to see Charlie all the time and find out what life with him permanently would be like. And it looked to me like it would be good!

As far as sleeping arrangements, oh, of course we had separate rooms. Waiting until I was married to have sex was always something I was going to do. And his mum clearly thought the same, 'cause as soon as I was there she was like, 'You're to sleep with my Patti'. There was no running backwards and forwards between bedrooms in those days. People just never got up to things like that then. It was a good thing in a way.

Actually I say that, but obviously some people did still get up to stuff, 'cause I remember there would be whisperings from time to time about someone who had been 'confined' even though she wasn't married. That's what they called it when you got pregnant – 'she's been confined'. Confined to what I don't know! But that's what it was. I remember my nan always said that, and it was sort of said with a little gasp, as though talking about being pregnant was a bit of a naughty secret. As though by saying you were pregnant, even if you were married, it was like everyone knew you had done 'the deed'. But sometimes it was all kept under wraps. Like if a young girl was pregnant and not married, she would suddenly be sent away with no one being told, then come back seven months later.

'Where you been?'

'Oh, I've been down to stay with my aunt for a while,' or 'I've been working away for a bit, just to get a change of scene.' Or something like that.

But then the aunt would appear and she'd be carrying a baby.

'Oh, it's my aunt's baby, it's not . . .'

You wouldn't have kept the baby yourself. It would have just been too shameful, I suppose. It was never seen as possible, or an option as something you could do like they do today. You just wouldn't do it.

Anyway, by early February 1955, and two months since I had had any contact with my dad, we decided it was time me and Charlie went round and tried to talk to him. Although he had known Charlie's address, he had never come round, so we had no idea what kind of response we were going to get. Luckily I think he was pleased to see us – but there was no moving him on the topic of marriage. And the problem was that at that point you still had to be twenty-one to get married without your parent's permission. I was still only nineteen.

I had taken the consent form with me, and I put it in front of my dad, and I asked him, 'Will you sign this form, Dad?' and he said no. I really tried to coax him into it, but he just kept shaking his head. Then Charlie tried explaining it to him, and he looked at him with this fierce stare.

'No, she's not going to get married,' he said. 'She's not getting married at all.' As stubborn as all that, he was. And it was clear we weren't going to get anywhere with him.

'Dad, we're going to get married eventually anyway,' I said, hoping that would make him see sense. 'So please won't you just agree?'

'Well, if you do, I won't give you away,' he said coldly.

I know he thought he was being a good dad looking out for his daughter, but it didn't feel like he was really thinking about my happiness. He didn't have any real reason to object to Charlie and while I can't blame him for not wanting to be on his own, it was also a bit of a power game, and was selfish of him too, the way he was acting.

I begged and pleaded with him, until it was clear it was no use. And I left there in tears and said to Charlie, 'It looks like we really can't get married yet.' I wouldn't be twenty-one until the November of the year after, so we had a long wait to do it without needing consent. So I decided it was no use for the time being, and moved back in with my dad.

I stopped trying to discuss it with him, and we kind of lived an awkward limbo life, where we didn't ignore each other, but conversation was even less than before. There was like this tension in both of us, that meant we were both angry and not backing down.

Then I went and saw my brother, who I hadn't seen for a good few months, and told him about it, and could he talk with Dad? But he was no use.

'He won't take notice, you know how Dad is,' Tommy said. 'You know he won't change his mind on it.'

I was annoyed because he knew how much of a hard time I was having with him at home on my own – he had seen when he was there that life with Dad wasn't easy.

Then we had a little bit of an argument about it and I got so angry I went, 'Don't bother coming to the wedding then.' So that was it. I'd fallen out with both Tommy and my dad. Not a nice situation at all.

And I went through some right heartache over whether to marry Charlie after that. I really gave some serious thought to not marrying him, and giving in to my dad. At times it didn't seem like the fighting was worth it, and despite everything, he was still my dad, and I didn't want us to be hating each other.

But then I thought, what life have I got? This is my chance to be really happy. Do I honestly want to be stuck at home for the rest of my life, looking after the house for my dad? Besides, he was still dating that woman, and I thought there was every chance she was going to become his next wife, and I knew I didn't want to be living with her. And it also meant he would have less need of me.

So we pushed on with our plans to get engaged and went and chose a ring for me. We didn't have the money for anything fancy, so we went to a pawn shop in Canning Town and that's where I got my ring. I've worn it now for fifty-five years. And someone had owned it before me, so imagine how old it is! It's worn down a lot in that time I have to say.

Then we started getting ready for the wedding. We decided we would push on with it, and another family member agreed to sign the consent form instead. We all knew it would annoy my dad, but we'd decided to go for it, so tough.

Me and Charlie had £50 saved up between us, so we decided we would use that to pay for the wedding, and we arranged to have it just the next month, on 19 March 1955. None of this two years of planning or whatever people take today! I had five bridesmaids, just different people from around where Charlie lived and friends of Charlie's family. Two of them were little girls, only about five years old at the time: Margaret Morrison, who lived next door to Charlie in Canning Town, at number 7 Bray Drive, and Linda, who was his sister Mary's little girl.

And I remember talking to a friend of mine at work called Joycie. She had got married a year before I did, and I said to her one day, 'I've got to go and get a dress, ain't I?'

'Don't buy one. Try my dress on first before you get one,' she said.

I tried on the dress she had got married in, which was white and lace and beautifully traditional, and it fitted me lovely. So I borrowed her frock to get married in, and her veil, so all I had to go and buy for myself were the shoes.

Then I got a woman round the corner to make up the bridesmaid dresses for me. I remember I got the material from a stall that there used to be in Upton Park, over East Ham way. I bought a lot of pink material off them that cost half a crown a yard. It was a lot of money in them days, though I suppose that is nothing by today's standards. She had some material left at the finish, and just 'cause the war was over, you still weren't wasteful. So she went to me, 'Have you flowers?' and when I said no she turned the rest of it into muffs for the bridesmaids to wear instead. She was a clever lady with a needle and thread that woman.

I had tried to ask Dad to come one more time. It was a couple of evenings before the big day when the two of us were sat at home in silence. I knew the answer would be no, but I needed to try, to give him a chance to change his mind. I said to him, 'Come on then, it's almost my wedding. Please will you come?' But he just said, 'I bet it'll never last, and you'll come running back to me. Anyway, I'm already going to a wedding that day so I won't be able to come.'

On the same day, one of the daughters or granddaughters of the woman he was courting was getting married and he decided to go to that instead, as though she was more important to him than me. It was so mean. I thought, 'Oh, please', and was so sad about it. I never cried at that time, though, I just felt it inside, like a hurt in my stomach. I never forgave him for it, if I'm honest. I think it was one of the nastiest things a dad can do to his daughter, and for no reason other than his own stubbornness.

We got married at St Luke's church on Jude Street, just a couple of streets away from Charlie's home. It was a beautiful big old church, really lovely and impressive inside and outside. It was a man called Father Goose who did the service. I loved that name, always made me laugh!

We met him a bit before the service, and as I hadn't gone to church there before, I had to go a couple of times on a Sunday in the weeks before the wedding.

Charlie had someone he knew from the pub who had a car, and he offered to drive me to the church in it. Although it was so close to their home, it wouldn't do to make me walk the streets in my wedding dress. Charlie and his brother Dickie, who was his best man, just walked round, as it wasn't so bad for the groom to have to walk. Bit easier in his outfit. Charlie wore his demob suit – the suit you get when you leave the armed forces. They give you vouchers to go and get yourself a suit, to help set you up in the civvy world, and the one he had bought he wore to our wedding. It didn't matter to me that he had worn it before, he still looked handsome, I can tell you!

On the day, neither my dad or Tommy came as expected, so I was on my own when I got married, with no one from my own family to give me away. The job went to my mother-in-law's boyfriend instead. And Aunt Alice – remember her, with the fur collar? – and her husband Uncle Stan signed as witnesses and did all the necessary paperwork. My dad found out afterwards, and he was none too happy with them, but by then it was done.

I found out recently the church is still there, but it isn't a church any more, it's a business centre. Terrible isn't it – still a beautiful old building, but with all sorts of offices inside, and even a doctor's surgery. Seems you can get just about anything in there these days – except a marriage! It did make me kind of sorry to see that happen to it.

Then, after we were officially married, we had the reception back at Charlie's mother's house. You'd never have hired a reception venue then, you'd never have afforded it. No, instead we were doing everything ourselves the night before. We made boiled bacon sandwiches – I remember that clear as day – just working away to get enough of them ready for the next day, while being all excited like.

Then we decided the house didn't look clean enough, and we were scrubbing the place out, and I remember my sister-in-laws there with paintbrushes, repainting the kitchen! Oh, it was great really. We pulled together, a real team effort to get it all done in time. Not that the men helped. I have no idea where they were. Probably on the settees or down the pub, but it wouldn't have been expected in them days for them to help out.

So after the church, everyone came back to Charlie's mum's place for the reception, and we had a wedding cake there that we had bought. It was a pathetic little thing really when I look back, but it was all we could afford. I was just glad to have one.

We had lots of beer and spirits as well as the food. In fact, I think that is the most expensive bit of the wedding, what we mostly spent our savings on. And oh yes, did the men make the most of it. So much so that do you know what? Even though I had been saving myself for Charlie on our wedding night . . . I had to wait another night. Going to bed for our first time together that night? There was no way it was going to happen! The bugger got so drunk that he passed out sat up on the settee and slept down there. Oh, I remember that . . . and I teased him about it ever since.

I think all the men were so drunk, to be honest, they all passed out on the settees. And I wasn't a lover of drink all that much, so I was sober, and us girls ended up clearing up around them. I wasn't best pleased, but that's how it was.

Then after a while Charlie's mum waved a hand at us to go to bed. That's all she had to do, she had a real control over her household did my mum-in-law, she just waved a hand and we all headed off to bed.

And, that night, my wedding night, I shared my bed with his two sisters and his brother's wife. All four of us in the same bed! I can't see that happening today or people putting up with it – not exactly what you expect on your wedding night, is it?

As for Charlie, he told me he woke up the next day and thought, 'Well, I can't remember, but I must have got drunk. Now where am I? And am I getting married today, or did I get married yesterday?' Oh, he was bad 'un!

Even years later my kids used to sit there and say, 'Dad, how could you do that to poor Mummy on her honeymoon?' and you know what he'd say? 'Well, at least she always had what I've got later on.' Oh, I tell you . . . he was a rascal!

But it was all change the next night – we made that our wedding night. I was nervous, I tell you – remember all those stories my nan had filled my head with when I was younger? Even with Gracie telling me things, I didn't really know what was what and what wasn't. But I needn't have worried myself!

There was one other good thing I discovered the day after our wedding, though, that allowed me to get some secret revenge on Charlie. Despite us setting aside £50 to cover the wedding, and thinking we would still be tight up with that, we didn't even use it all. We still had change from the £50! Not that I told Charlie. I kept that to myself, as a little present.

Anyway, after our wedding we were off on our honeymoon. We went to Leysdown on the Isle of Sheppey and stayed in a rented caravan. My sister-in-law and her husband and two boys, Ronnie and Georgie, came on the honeymoon too, in the next caravan over. That might sound strange, but it wasn't rare in them days.

It was a very relaxed honeymoon. I remember just going for walks, relaxing on the beach and playing games, or heading into town to look around the shops. It was a lovely time, and after that we made a point of going back to Leysdown as often as we could. Years later, as we got more money together, we even bought our own caravan down there rather than renting every time. Nothing fancy mind, but just something that did us fine. I lived and died on the Isle of Sheppey, as they say!

FIFTEEN

Sugar Girl

After we got married and came home from the honeymoon, I went back to living with my mother-in-law, but this time on a more permanent basis. Now it was my home too, I wasn't just a temporary guest.

Bray Drive was a kind of little cul-de-sac of council houses, down near Victoria Docks, a couple of miles away from Devons Road. A little bit of an alley out the back of the road would take you practically straight down to the docks. I never went down there, as I always thought of them as a bit dirty and rough. How close they were definitely had an influence on people in the area. Most people had some link to the docks and the ships that would come and go from there, or some member of their family working on them. As an area, it was working class again, not that different to Devons Road, and most people were friendly and just getting on with their lives.

Our house was third from the end on Bray Drive, on the left as you turned into it. It was a little grey brick terraced house over two floors, with three bedrooms. When I moved in, Charlie's mum had the main room, me and Charlie had another, and the third was for any of the other kids or grandkids who happened to be staying round at that point.

There was a little bit of a garden out back, with an outside toilet, although his mum had also had a new inside one built too. She used to use the outside one in the day, and the inside one at night, so no night visits to the garden. But after a bit of time we turned the outside toilet into a shed. That was probably the fate of most outside toilets in the end.

To get in the front of the house, you had to open a little gate, then there was a tiny pathway to the door. I guess for me it was a step up in the world, mainly 'cause it was a house not a flat.

There were some right characters in that street for neighbours, as I remember. Next door was Margaret Morrison, who as I say was my bridesmaid, and her mum. They were nice people. But then the other side of them was a lady, I forget her name – Mrs Duffield – I think. She was nice enough, but oh, she had so many children. And then her eldest daughter lived just a few doors further along, and she had loads of kids as well, so that between them you didn't know whose was whose. The children were always running around and swapping between the two houses. I think the two women must have shared looking after them, so that the bedrooms of each house were jointly used for all their kids. For one day it seemed the boys were in one bedroom in one house, and the next they were swapping with the girls in the other. It was all a bit crazy, but they seemed to pull it off, and were happy enough. I guess they were like the Armitage family back in my old block in Bilberry House. When your family is that big, all the normal rules can't apply for how you do things. You jumble through the best way you can.

Then on the corner across the way was a copper, who we nicknamed Nosey Nobby the bobby. And oh, I didn't like him. He was like one of those self-important men who had got a little bit of power, and needed to use it to its full effect to make everyone notice him. He always paid attention to what everyone in Bray Drive was doing – and interfered in it wherever he could. He was a devil he was. My Charlie used to say, 'One of these days I'm gonna give him such a good hiding!' Nosey Nobby used to wind him up rotten. It was terrible really. But everyone thought the same – they used to talk about 'that horrible man' and you'd know they were talking about our copper friend. No one liked him down our road.

Then a couple of doors down from him was a woman known as Well-off Kate – but I will come back to her later 'cause she had a more important role to play for us than just a friendly neighbour.

Mostly, though, I liked the street, although it didn't have quite the same community feel that Bilberry House had. People did talk and still help each other and what have you, but people weren't in and out of each other's homes all the time, invited or not! And there were no big events like the Queen's Jubilee, or the end of the war, that made everyone organize big parties in the road or what have you, which might have pulled people together more. Everyone was just too busy working and making their way through life best they could, I think.

But yeah, other than me moving into the same bedroom as Charlie, generally life continued pretty much as it had done when I had stayed there before while we were courting. We were both still working, I would come home of a night and do things at home, and me and Charlie got on just as well.

Charlie's dad had left years before and had no contact with them. I don't think Charlie even knew a thing about him: his name, where he had gone to, or anything. But the mother-in-law had remarried soon after, and she and Charlie's step-dad had a daughter, so Patti was his half-sister really. And as I understand it, that man was more a father to Charlie than his real one. He brought up the three kids that weren't his too, Mary, Dickie and Charlie. But he had died before I met Charlie, so I never got to meet him.

The mother-in-law was not short of attention and had plenty of boyfriends, generally navy men. She wasn't especially beautiful, she had a pretty face but she was quite a large woman. But she had a way about her that seemed to appeal to the men. And she worked for years down on the docks cleaning the boats and I think that is where she met a lot of the men. I'm not sure she ever really found anyone who replaced her husband, though, and she never seemed to stick with any of them too long.

As for actually living with her, well maybe it was because she was cleaning at work, but she never done much of it at home. Like she'd get in and go to me, 'You cleaned up in here today? Them windows want cleaning', and all that business, even when they were clean.

But she wasn't too bad really. It was just that it was her house and she was in charge, and she wanted everyone to remember that. But that's how it was in them days. I wouldn't have questioned it. No, I had a lot of time for her. Like everyone, we had our ups and downs and little arguments here and there, but that was it. We never sat down to have deep and meaningful conversations, and I'd never say she was a close friend, but we worked well together in a kind of companionable way.

Her real name was Nell Brooker, but some days I called her Mum, if I was feeling close to her and we had been getting on especially well, or mother-in-law when I described her to other people – or when we weren't getting on so well!

She and Charlie were very close. I suppose with the dad having left them, he had felt more responsibility for looking after his mum than a lot of lads might do. He was a proper grafter was Charlie. It was in him from a young age to work hard for his money, and he always made sure his mum was well looked after. Yeah, he was always very good to her. One of the things I always used to admire in him was his protectiveness of her. All the kids were good to her really, but it was Charlie I saw properly take on the man's role in her life.

It was in Bray Drive that me and Charlie became proud owners of our first television set. It was a tiny little black-and-white thing, but I did enjoy it. I had a few favourite shows that I watched over the years, but the old ones set in East London generally caught my eye the most. Like *Steptoe and Son*, I loved that show. Those two old rag-and-bone men, and that old boy on his horse and cart . . . oh, you'll never get shows like that back again.

And *Dixon of Dock Green*, that old police show set over this way, that was pretty popular too. I guess the

East End was a good setting for shows. There was so much happening in the place and so much history and things that people wanted to get their teeth into. Like Jack the Ripper, that story always fascinates people. All under the arches, and dark and scary . . . it plays on your imagination.

By now, I had swapped where I was working – no more smelly sack factory for me, thank you very much! And this time I found a place I stayed for some time. Don't get me wrong, not because of any great sense of loyalty to the company, but because it was a place that treated their workers that bit better, so for a nice life, you actually wanted to stay there.

It was the Tate & Lyle factory on Factory Road in Silvertown, which produced bags of sugar. Tate & Lyle was a step up from the other factories I had worked in until that point. It was more like the bigger, more efficient factories of the future, and felt like a well-oiled machine in how it ran, rather than a workshop in the back of a converted garage.

Say for things like your lunch, in the other factories production was stopped while everyone had a break at the same time. This is not what happened at Tate & Lyle. There you always had someone to take your place, and it was all shift work, so production never stopped. It was the only factory in London that worked twenty-four hours round the clock, seven days a week, even Christmas. This meant it was better pay, and you had a bit of flexibility too to choose the hours that worked for you.

My main job there was getting the sugar into bags. You never got a moment to stop, you were on the go all the time because piles and piles of that sugar just kept coming round and round on this conveyor belt, needing to be dealt with, while us women stood alongside it and got stuck in. It was the everyday cane sugar that goes in your tea, in cakes, wherever.

But one week out of every month we all had to do a different job – bagging up the icing sugar. And oh, that was a nightmare. Even though it was more money, it was the one job that no one wanted to do – everyone would try their luck with the foreman, like, 'Let so and so get on it, not me this time!' It was so powdery, it would get up your nose, in your eyes, you'd be covered in it . . . This day and age, you'd have a mask on, but not then. You'd literally be in a cloud of this stuff, breathing it in so you could taste the sweetness in your mouth and throat, but you still had to work and get on with it. I'm sure it can't have been good for you.

One thing I did make sure I got up to was more smuggling, but this time I learned from my mistakes in Yardley's and was more careful. My mum had got away with it for years with her sweets in her turban, so I wasn't about to give up – it was the only way I could give myself a bonus!

You were always searched on the way out – there was an acceptance that the workers would pinch stuff if we could, and the bosses weren't prepared to take the loss. So pockets, handbags, etc., were searched, generally by the forelady. A full body pat down if they felt it necessary! But me and my friends made sure we hid the sugar where we wouldn't get searched. No more turban hiding for us. No. Instead we used to have these tiny little bags that we would fill with the sugar and put down our bras. You wouldn't take a lot, but sugar was expensive and still in high demand in them days – if you could get it at all. A left-over from rationing days, I suppose, 'cause sugar rationing only stopped in September 1953 so it was still pretty fresh in our minds. So we'd make sure we got our share that way.

I'm sure everyone in the factory was at it really, it was just seen as a bit of a perk of the job. Most workers in most factories across the country at that time were probably giving themselves those little bonuses! When you're hard up, you have to put some effort into thinking of ways to ease the hardship of surviving. And when you were on such a low salary, well, it was seen as fair game.

Anyway, of an evening I'd get home from work, and still have to do all the jobs a woman had to do in the house. Every man at that time had to have his dinner on the table when he walked in from work, no matter what. So that was always priority. The attitude in them days was a man was very much a man and a woman was a woman. The man was in charge, whereas her job was the home, and that was that. It wasn't something that was an option or could be questioned, it's just how it was.

And a man would moan as often as not about things at home, no matter how good they were – 'my shirt isn't well ironed', 'these potatoes are cooked funny', 'what's that dust on the shelf?' – they moaned for the sake of it, we used to think! Nowadays most girls would say, 'Well if you don't like it, do it yourself', and fight back that way. But then you bit your tongue and let it wash over you. Besides, I wasn't that keen on going out, and there wasn't that much else to do, so getting on and doing the work indoors was as good as anything.

I was also starting to enjoy cooking a lot more, and would try out a few more dishes when I could, although everything was very traditional compared with today. It was meat or fish and veg. But I started adding things like stews and different pies into our food for the week. And I also tried cooking with eels.

Although we'd always been big on seafood in my family, for some reason we'd only ever seen jellied eels and the likes in the shop, I'd never made them myself. And I know a lot of people not from the East End turn their noses up at eels, but you really shouldn't. They are a great dish, and so simple to make as well. I love doing them stewed or jellied. They are proper nutritious and filling as well. Give it a go! There's my favourite recipe on page 303 for you to follow.

Moneywise we were doing ok at this time. We weren't earning enough to put anything away for the future, but we were getting by and that was our main aim. Not so with my mother-in-law. It wasn't that she didn't earn enough, it was that she had a fondness for treating herself to things she couldn't really afford. And her way to be able to do this? The tallyman. If you don't know who that is, the best I can think of describing him is like an early credit card, or a bank loan.

It was like money lending, but from an individual, not a bank, and you just sort of paid him a little bit back of what you had borrowed each week. The tallyman never lent you huge amounts, like thousands or anything, it was more like ten or twenty pounds, although that was worth a lot more then that it is now, of course. Then he'd write it in his book and come back and knock on your door each week. You gave him what you could afford, like a shilling or a couple of coppers, there was no set amount, and they'd write it down and I suppose work out your interest. I don't think the interest was that high, but I don't know for sure – maybe that's just the impression the tallyman wanted me to have!

Anyway, this one time I had my sister-in-law Mary's little girl Linda with me – I was looking after her while her mum was out – and we spotted the tallyman coming down the road. He was always smartly dressed in a suit and always carried this posh-looking briefcase with him. He would come around every Friday to collect his money, and you could almost see everyone shrinking back from their curtains, and thinking up their excuses not to pay that week.

'Go out there,' my mother-in-law said this one time – like she said most weeks if I'm honest – 'and tell him I'm not in. I don't want to pay this week.'

'Alright then,' I said and opened the door and went out. I was just going to say she wasn't in, when the little 'un scurried past me and said, 'My nan said she ain't in.' Oh, I'll never forget that! I can still see it now.

'Take no notice of her,' I said to the tallyman, hoping I looked honest. 'She's not in, she's gone out somewhere.' Then I told Linda, 'Go on in, you naughty girl.'

'No, she didn't go out,' the cheeky so-and-so carried on. 'But Nanny says she ain't in.'

I'm sure the kid thought she was helping, but I was dying of embarrassment on the doorstep, and so was my mother-in-law, who was standing in the front room just yards away from the door, listening to the whole conversation. The tallyman laughed, though, and noted it down in his book. I'm sure he was used to hearing every excuse under the sun, so nothing was new to him. Probably meant extra interest anyway, as far as he was concerned.

I never used the tallyman, tempting though it was sometimes. But I was always quite sure about just spending what we actually had. It was something I had seen my parents do, stick tightly within a budget, and Charlie was strict in his mind about doing the same.

But I can see why people did turn to the tallyman. And to tell the truth, more people did it than not really. Often it wasn't 'cause they had overspent on spoiling themselves, it was 'cause they had no choice. If their husbands were out of work, you didn't get money from the social. It was a sad state of affairs, but I think a lot of people, especially after the war, were running permanently in debt and they could never get out of it.

There were some benefits you could get then if you were out of work, but nothing like the range there is today, and what you got was so small that no one would ever sit back and rely on it. The general thinking was you either worked for it or you got nothing, whereas today some people are better off on benefits than going to work. It's pathetic! I don't think there should be dole. I went on to raise all my children and both Charlie and I worked and we kept our kids without help from anyone. We were always in work, and that is how it should be. But I know, I know, things have changed.

Around this time I have to admit, however, I did develop a habit that I suppose you could tell me was one way to waste my money – I started smoking. I had never tried smoking when I was young, and it wasn't something I was that interested in, but Charlie smoked, and over time I just picked up the habit off him. It was something I did because he did it, and then it went from there. I only smoked about five a day at the most – even since then it's never been a lot unless I'm in company. Then it is a different matter – if someone goes, 'Here, have a cigarette' I have one and then it's like I have another and another . . .

I smoked Wills Woodbine cigarettes back then, while Charlie had his tobacco pouch and used to roll them up himself.

Smoking and drinking really were the only vices that existed them days, or only as I know of anyway. Not that alcohol had started to appeal to me any more than it had when I was younger. So it was just smoking that was my vice.

I never knew anyone who took drugs, I didn't really even know there was such a thing. If I had seen someone in the street on drugs I most probably would have thought they were drunk, but I'm pretty sure most of the time that is what it was. The only thing I suppose could have been people addicted to prescription drugs, but that wouldn't have been a thing that would have been talked about, so no one would have known. No really, it was all about the alcohol and the tobacco.

And I was quickly learning that alcohol was a habit that was high on my husband's list. A bit like my dad, though, it wasn't so much about the actual alcohol as the socializing that came with it.

So Charlie would like nothing better than to head off to the pub of a night, enjoy his few pints, and hold court with all the other men for a few hours. I can't say I was always happy about it, and it caused plenty of rows over the years, but in the early days I just shrugged and saw it as something he did 'cause he was a man, and I'd seen it all before with my dad. And don't get me wrong, it wasn't every night, weekends more than likely, but in the week it was more dependent on his mood.

No, I didn't mind it really at that time, but what I did used to get mad about was that he was going out, so it seemed there was one rule for him and a different one for me, and I didn't always like it! He wouldn't let me go nowhere on my own, but he could go anywhere he wanted. Oh, we had terrible rows about that.

Beanos were the perfect example of that. Charlie used to go on plenty of those still, but he wouldn't let me go on any of the ladies' ones once I was married. He hadn't liked me going on them before we were married, but I suppose he thought he couldn't tell me what to do then, but once I was his wife, he put his foot down. Once you were a married lady your place was in the home and all that. Oh, there were all sorts of rows over it. When I had a strong feeling or opinion on something, I would let Charlie know, so we did have some right old arguments in the early days, but he stood his ground, and mostly I eventually backed down just for an easier life. So I never got to go on no more beanos.

And, of course, the fact he was so against me going on them got my mind to wondering what happened on his beanos that he was so worried about me going on them. 'Cause you hoped your men behaved when they went off on their trips, and that they would come back to you at the end of it all, having had fun, but not having done anything they oughtn't have, but you can never know 100 per cent. I remember a few rows friends of ours had when the men came back with love bites on their necks. That was all the go then, love bites, and some of the men obviously got a bit carried away with girls they had met on the beanos.

But I trusted Charlie, 'cause you had to really, didn't you? Bit bleedin' late now anyway, ain't it! But I just thought he would be there having a laugh and a joke. If I let my mind wander when he was actually away for the day, I'd wonder what he was doing, and if he was courting anyone, but I didn't seriously think it. Ultimately he was a good husband and I trusted him. I had to.

So the beanos just carried on – off he headed on his day trips, pretty regular like, mostly to Southend like my dad used to, and then I think they had the odd trip to Margate. That was it, though, they never went further than that in a day. Probably a good thing, too!

SIXTEEN

A New Arrival

We hadn't been married that long before I fell pregnant with our first child. I suppose it was about seven months, me coming up to my twentieth birthday, when I realized I was expecting.

It wasn't something I had planned, and it was probably a bit earlier than I had thought I would have kids, but it weren't the end of the world or anything. I think I had pretty mixed emotions when I knew – I can honestly say I was both pleased and I wasn't, if that makes sense. I think mainly it was because I didn't know what to expect. You don't know, do you, unless you have been around pregnancy and new babies growing up, and I hadn't.

But I realized what was happening when I missed a period, and I told my sister-in-law Mary who said she thought I was pregnant and got all excited about it. I remember Mary, who already had children, telling me all about what would happen. And then Patti, who had married a year before me and was pregnant with Billy, her eldest son by the time of my wedding, well, she was telling me all about it too. She was especially excited that we were going to have kids so close together, so that there wouldn't be much age difference in the cousins and they could play together. I suppose motherhood, like most things, is nicer when you can share it with a friend.

Anyhow, before I told Charlie's mum, she guessed. We were sat there one day and I was getting up the courage to tell her, when she just said, 'What's the matter, girl? Ah, you're pregnant.' And she pointed at her nose.

'What's me nose got to do with it?' I went.

'It changes. The nose always gives it away when someone's expecting.'

Oh, shut up, woman, how can you know by a nose? I thought, but I kept that answer to myself! And true enough it seemed she was always right. I saw her predict so many pregnancies, and tap her nose every time. I could never spot a change myself, but I guess there must be something to it.

So to be sure I definitely was pregnant, I went to the doctor's and he made me do a urine test – or what we called a water test – and it came back that it was true. I was so scared, sat in his room, that I said, 'Please don't tell me I am, I'm not, am I?' But the doctor loved kids – I think he had about twenty of his own – and he was always so happy to tell someone they were expecting that he couldn't get the smile off his face as he told me. And I think once I got past being nervous, I was quite pleased really.

And, well, Charlie, he was proper happy he was going to be a dad when I came home from the doctor's and told him. He said it was the next natural thing now we were married, and he was sure we would have a good, big, healthy family. He loved the idea, and kept telling everyone he was going to be a dad.

One thing that made me sad about it, though, was that my own dad wasn't around to know he was expecting a grandchild. Me and him had not talked since I got married, after he didn't come to the wedding. I felt really sad and resentful, and I just think on his side he didn't want to admit he had been wrong.

He knew where I lived 'cause he had the address from when I had been courting Charlie and he had wanted to know where he lived. But he was stubborn, and would never come and apologize. And I never wanted to go and see him 'cause I was still angry with him. I felt it was down to him to patch things up. After all, in my eyes he was the one who had been in the wrong.

But after a while I thought to myself that it was never

going to happen. If a year on the man hadn't been around to see me, he probably never would. Besides, everyone loved a gossip then, so I was sure the fact I was expecting would have got back to him, and even that wasn't making him step down off his bleedin' high horse.

I would lie awake and cry at night sometimes, thinking to myself how I had no mum, and now I had no dad. It was bad enough to lose one, but now I had lost them both. And I'd imagine what it would be like to have had them both in my life still, which just made me even sadder. I especially thought about my mum, 'cause I suppose being pregnant is one of those times you feel you really want her there to help you and give you advice. But it was one of them things I could do nothing about, so I just got on with concentrating on my baby instead.

I found pregnancy fairly easy. I didn't get morning sickness or any bad symptoms and I just kept working at Tate & Lyle as late as possible. All the women did – you couldn't really afford to take more time off than you absolutely had to.

Being my first one, I decided I wanted to have the baby in hospital. I was nervous as could be about it, and thought I needed the nurses there and all that medical equipment about and all that, just for safety like.

By then they had started to put up phone boxes in

the street and you could make a call by putting a tuppence piece into the phone. People couldn't afford to make calls for general chats, though – phones were only used for important reasons, such as a call to the hospital. But closer to us than the nearest phone box was a different phone – one that belonged to the neighbour I mentioned before across the road called Well-off Kate. Her name was actually Nell Nyland, so I've no idea where the name Kate came from, and why she wasn't Well-off Nell, but she wasn't, no one questioned it, and Well-off Kate just stuck.

She was called that because as far as we were concerned, she was rich. And what was the main reason for thinking she was? She and her husband had a car. Nothing special mind – I forget exactly what it was – but they had a car. I think they were just about the only people in the area with one. And more importantly at this point, they also had a phone.

In fact they were the first people I knew to have a phone in their house. And Well-off Kate would allow people to use her phone – if they paid her. Well-off Kate's house was a lot closer than our nearest phone box, so it made more sense to go to hers. So you'd get a tuppenny bit, and go over there and ask if you could use the phone, and you'd call where you needed to – mostly it was the hospital, 'cause that was pretty much the only place anybody used to have to call – and then you'd put your coin in the box she had sat there, ready for your money.

The telephone was this great big thing with a dial on the front, where you had to put your finger in the hole for the number and pull it the whole way around. Then there was one earpiece that hung on the side of the phone that you held up to your ear to listen, and a separate one you held to speak into. A few years later Well-off Kate swapped it for what was considered a modern phone – one where the ear piece and speaker were all on the same handset, but at this time there were the two pieces.

Anyway, I started getting contractions on 22 June 1956 and this is when we put her phone to good use. Mary dashed over there and called for an ambulance. I remember it coming down our road, all blue lights flashing, and the neighbours' curtains twitching. And it took me to Plaistow Maternity Hospital on Howards Road. Of course, as seems to be the case with every other hospital in the East End, it has since closed down – I think it's housing now. But then it was the main hospital in the area for women having babies.

'Cause it was my first time, a midwife explained to me what was going to happen, then they put me in a hot shower, put a hat on me and then shaved me underneath like – they did everything for me. I don't suppose you get all that done for you now, do you?

Then I went into labour properly like. Looking back I don't think I knew what was going to happen at all. There wasn't the same information around then as there is now – TV shows about maternity wards, magazines articles about giving birth, antenatal classes to teach you and your husband how to get through the birth together . . . no, there was not a hope in hell of any of that. The little knowledge I did have came from my sisters-in-law having told me some things, but there was a lot they had obviously held back on.

I really didn't know what to expect. The birth seemed to go on for ever, and it weren't fun, I'll be honest. There weren't all these pain-relieving things back then neither. All I had was gas and air, and that was it. I never had to have any stitches, though, and that was something I was pleased about.

Charlie came up to the hospital with me when I first went, but he didn't stay for the birth. It's not like nowadays when half the husbands are in the delivery room. Then I don't think any of them did that. You might have had your mother or sister in the room with you and the midwife, but that would have been it.

If they'd asked if I wanted Charlie in when I was in the pain of giving birth, I think my answer would have been more like, 'Get him away, I am suffering and he has done this to me!' Ha, none of this shared experience stuff for me, thank you very much.

And finally I gave birth to a baby girl. Not that I got to see her when she came out, she was whisked off straightaway. They took her off to give her a slap and get her breathing right, and to clean her up. Then they kept her away for a couple of hours, as was the way then, to let the mother recover properly first. Not like today, when the baby pops out and is on the mother's chest immediately.

I couldn't wait for my little baby to come back, though. It was a great feeling to hold her for the first time, as any mum'll tell you. Again, I did wish my own mum could have been there to share the moment with me.

Then I had to stay in hospital for fourteen days, not 'cause anything went wrong, but just 'cause that was the normal way things were done then. You weren't allowed to get up for the first ten days after giving birth, then day twelve you could get up and walk around, and day fourteen you could leave, assuming everything had gone well. Nowadays people seem to have a baby one hour, and leave hospital the next!

We decided to call the baby June because, well, we were trying to figure out what to call her, and she was born in June, and we weren't sure what else to go for so that was as good a name as any!

It was a scary day, leaving hospital with her for the first time. The nurses had shown me how to do most things, but once you leave, you are on your own. I'm sure every new mum knows that feeling, although you soon get into the flow of how you do everything. Generally I think I did ok as a new mum, I just got on with it. You just had to, I suppose. There was nothing else you could do. And Charlie was so pleased with the birth of his first child – he couldn't stop grinning about it, and telling people.

As far as all the equipment went, like a cot and pushchairs and baby clothes, they were mostly handed on from friends or my sisters-in-law. Everyone would pass all those kinds of things between each other. No sense in spending money to get it for new when you could ill afford to.

Although she was a good baby, she was a bit of a crier was June. I seemed to spend forever comforting her, and not being sure what was wrong. I was always taking her up to the hospital to try and find out if something was actually physically wrong with her, 'cause especially being a mum for the first time, you worry even more than you might do normally. But no matter how much I fed her or rocked her, or left her to try and sleep, she would cry.

And at first when they checked her out, they said they thought she had a hole in the heart. Oh, that was tough to hear, that was. Not something you want to hear about your kid. It right upset me, and she was in and out of this children's hospital in Hackney while they tried to get to the bottom of it.

But then they decided her heart was fine, so goodness knows where they had got that from in the first place. And they couldn't find anything else wrong with her. So in the end I was told she was one of those babies that cry for everything, and I would have to get used to it! I couldn't do anything else other than accept what they said. But, oh, the sleepless nights I used to spend up with June. Looking back, those early days were not easy – it's a wonder I went on to put myself through it four more times, truthfully!

A couple of months after June was born, I went back to work at Tate & Lyle. There was no such thing as maternity pay or anything like that, so having a kid instantly meant we had less money coming in, and then soon after, an extra mouth to feed, so staying off work wasn't an option. Family allowance money from the government had been started by now, but you didn't get any money for your first child, so I didn't even have any help on that front, so it wasn't like I could take a year off or anything.

Even unpaid maternity leave didn't exist either. To go and have a baby, you pretty much had to hand your notice in and hope for the best. Then when you wanted to go back to work, you just had to see if there was anything going, and hope the old place wanted you still. And luckily for me, Tate & Lyle wanted me back.

Although Charlie's brother and sisters had left home by now, his sisters in particular might have still lived at home. They were round a lot, and often stayed over with the kids. Mary in particular was there all the time, more than she was at her own house. She worked at Tate & Lyle too and we got quite a good system going. Because of the shift work, you had a choice of working lots of different hours, but I remember the main ones were six in the morning until two, two until ten, or ten until six, plus various weekend options. We never did the night shifts or weekends, but one of us would always do the early shift of a day, and one the later one, and whoever wasn't working would look after the other one's kids as well as their own. It sounds complicated, but it wasn't!

We'd do it week about, so one week I'd be up and at work at six o'clock, and the next week starting at two o'clock. That way we never had to pay anyone to look after our kids, which, to be honest, we couldn't have afforded. But nor could we have afforded not to work. For the hour or so around two o'clock when the kids did have to be left on their own, while one of us was leaving to get to work and the other was leaving work to come home, we'd get a girl from nearby or a neighbour to come in and look after them for us. Then we'd treat her, give her a couple of bob, or a couple of coppers.

Charlie took to fatherhood well, although being a dad was a different kind of role in them days. They weren't expected to be so hands on like, it was more a case of them being there to bring home money and to discipline the kids when they needed it. So he wasn't like some fathers today, like he wouldn't have changed their napkins and all that business. But sometimes he'd be like, 'Change her and then I'll look after her', then he'd take his turn holding June for a bit.

But really he was busy working all hours God could give him. He was doing a bit of everything and anything, because in them days you done it all you know. There was none of these set nine to five jobs, with paid time off and what have you, or turning down a job because you don't fancy it. Then you took everything you could.

I can remember Charlie doing quite a bit down at the docks around this time, helping out with maintaining the boats, and loading and unloading. There was an incredible amount of goods always arriving and leaving on those boats, and it would be loaded on and off of the trains that ran right to the docks, to be moved on elsewhere. But he also did things like help move barrels in the local pub one night a week for a few bob, and he helped out at a local butcher sometimes. As I say, anything and everything.

Anyway, at that time, what he brought home, added to what I was earning from working too, was what we needed in order to survive. If one of us had stopped working the amount we did, we'd have found ourselves falling into debt, and that was something we had promised ourselves we wouldn't do.

Charlie always used to say, 'Whatever you want, pay for it straightaway, I'm not having anything on the tick' – that's what you used to call it when you got something you promised to pay for bit by bit over future weeks, with a bit of interest added on of course. Kind of the same thinking I'd had in avoiding the tallyman. And that's how we went on, and I think it worked for us.

And instead of always buying things, I'd try to make June's clothes from time to time to make things easier, but it was so time-consuming. So I only did it when she was very little, just straight up and down little dresses, or ones with a bit of flare. Anything else would take you hours, and I just didn't have the time – or the patience! Although I did try and keep up the embroidery on pillows and tablecloths that my mum had taught me to do as a child. I enjoyed that more.

I never went out at all at this time. I have never really been one for going out anyway, but after June was born that was it, even trips to the cinema or to see a friend were pretty much out of the window. Where I'd mostly stayed home of an evening anyway, just with the odd evening out with Charlie, now I always stayed home. Until my twenty-first birthday that is. It was my birthday in November, five months after June was born. Charlie suggested that we get his mum to look after June for us that evening, and we'd go out by ourselves to the cinema. I was a bit worried about leaving June, but excited to go to the pictures 'cause it had been a long time since we'd had a night to us, so we decided to go for it.

He'd already spoiled me that day with the most lovely present of a necklace. It was gold and spells my name, Patricia. I was really happy with it and thought it was beautiful. I didn't own a lot of jewellery and I treasured what I did have. And do you know what, he put that necklace on me at twenty-one, and I haven't taken it off since, I even sleep in it. Whenever anyone tries to take it off me, I tell them, 'My Charlie put that necklace on my neck, and that's where he meant it to stay, so that's where it's staying.' I know people think I'm daft, but it's how I feel about it.

So anyway, that day we left June with the mum-in-law and headed off to see some film or another. It was a good evening, and we got a chance to relax together, just the two of us, for the first time in a long time. I'd forgotten how nice it had been when we were courting, and you could just joke about and have a laugh, and not worry about things in the house what needed to be done.

But however nice the evening was, it all got ruined when we got back to the house. Or rather, not even to the house, but as we turned into our road, for standing outside the front door we could see the mum-in-law standing holding a screaming baby, and scowling at us. Apparently dear Juney had screamed her head off pretty much from the minute we left until the minute we were home again. I remember she literally flung June at me and stormed off. Funnily enough the mum-in-law wasn't up for volunteering for babysitting duties again, and I never went out no more after that! Although actually, that's a bit of a lie – she was forced to look after her again just two days later, but it wasn't exactly for me to go off and have some fun.

I remember I had been getting stomach pains around then, but had been trying to ignore them. But suddenly they got really bad just after my birthday and I nearly fainted, and they were forced to call a doctor out. Then I was rushed to Poplar Hospital and it turned out I had appendicitis. So I had to stay in the hospital for an operation, and I had my appendix removed – so while I was there the mum-in-law had to look after June all over again!

Charlie wouldn't have looked after a baby on his own. He'd hold her and that when I was in the same room, but the actual looking after a kid wasn't seen as a man's role, it was part of the woman's role, part of looking after everything indoors. But I was happy with that. I enjoyed being a mother, and didn't envy him his long hours working to bring in money.

That time with appendicitis is about the only time I have got properly ill, touch wood. And that was especially lucky in them days 'cause there were so many awful illnesses going around. The biggest one in East London at that time was TB, tuberculosis. That was a killer, a real killer. When you got it then, you more than likely thought you would die. It was like cancer is today – the illness that is so common and that you really dread getting. And it spread so easily between people. Anywhere you were in close contact with people you risked getting it 'cause it travels through the air, when people sneeze, or cough, or spit or whatever.

I remember a tarmac factory near ours where there was a real epidemic of it. Maybe you were breathing a lot working there 'cause it was manual work and that, and then you'd breath in someone else's germs, and the TB was passed on. It was awful, but luckily it avoided the factories where I was.

And 'cause paper tissues you'd throw away weren't in use like they are today – then everyone carried cotton handkerchiefs – there were all sorts of safety notes on how to deal with the disposing of – sorry to say this – your phlegm.

I remember visiting an old man with TB, and he was sat there in front of his open fire, cough cough cough, and then spitting into the fire. That's what they told you to do, burn it, burn the germ out of it. And that's what people did, spit into the fire and put coal over it, and burn it away. I don't know if it worked, but that's what you did before tissues were around!

SEVENTEEN

Mrs Winky

A year after June was born, I was sitting in our front room with her on my lap, feeling a bit worried 'cause I was realizing it might have been a good few weeks since I'd had my period, and I was trying to do the maths.

I looked up and the mum-in-law was sat in her seat across from me, studying me closely. She had this same chair that she always sat in, that allowed her to have command of the whole room. She sat there sometimes and waved her arms around, and we would all just leap and do as she said. She had a certain manner that reminded everyone she was the boss, and we never forgot it!

Anyway, she leaned forward and looked at me, then just tapped her nose. 'Expecting again, aren't you?' she said.

'What you on about?' I went.

But she nodded, and sat back all satisfied.

At that point I still didn't believe her nose theory and would just write her off as having a mad old woman moment. But 'cause of the maths I had been doing just moments before . . . I took myself back to the doctor. And sure enough, I was pregnant again. Again Charlie was happy with the news. I was too, although I did wonder if we were having them too quick – we were still so young, and not earning that much money between us.

At least this time I knew what to expect from pregnancy, and although June was still only tiny so took a lot of attention, I felt I was coping. But I still decided I wanted to go back to Plaistow Maternity Hospital for the birth. In those days home births were pretty common, so I had that as a choice, but turned it down. And on 15 February 1959 I gave birth to a second daughter, Susan.

She was born tiny – six pounds – or at least that was considered too small in those days. I suppose it would be quite normal now, but then your baby had to be big and fat to be considered healthy! And I remember they put her in this huge incubator and gave her oxygen just to make sure she did fine. She had a little pink tag put on her 'cause that's what they done to show she needed looking after, and I've still got that saved, even today.

After the worries with June, I was scared I was going to have them again with Susan. She was so tiny, but it turned out there were no problems with her, and they let us out of the hospital soon after.

Again, after a couple of months, I went back to work, but I tell you, I was so busy at that time, I was run off my feet non-stop. Between the children and working at Tate & Lyle, and looking after the house and Charlie, I never got a moment's peace. If you look at any old photos, I am always in a turban like my mum had been years before, with my hair in rollers underneath it. I never ever had time to even have the rollers out and let my hair look nice or anything like that, so I just hid it away for ease! Worrying about my appearance was the last thing on my mind. It was all about practicality.

Being so tired, though, I was keen not to have any more babies too soon, so I started to think more about contraception. Now this is one thing that people take for granted these days, but back then, I can tell you it wasn't so easy at all. There were none of these pills and the like, there was nothing you could easily get your hands on to make your life easier. It was terrible!

No, the only thing you could use really was condoms, and even they were not easy to come by, I can tell you. Odd when you think about it. Nearly everyone must have needed them, but it was something you weren't supposed to talk about too much. A bit like the unmarried girls getting pregnant, it was too much like publicly announcing you were having sex. And that would never do.

I never saw condoms in the chemist – I haven't the foggiest if they sold them in there, but you never saw them out on display or anything. If they did sell them it was under the counter. So instead, you bought them from the barbers – come on now, obviously!

The men used to go and have their hair cut, then at the end when they were paying the barber would go, 'Anything for the weekend, sir?' by which he meant did they need condoms. And if the man said yes, it was like, 'One minute, sir' and they'd get a packet out of the till, along with the change for their haircut. That was how it was – haircut and some condoms!

But your husband wasn't going to go and get his hair cut every week, was he, so it was still a problem. And I knew that the more we kept risking not using them, the more likely I was to get pregnant, and I didn't want to be giving birth and getting pregnant again straightaway.

So it was bothering me, and I was thinking about it as I headed to Rathbone Market one day. Rathbone was an old street market in Canning Town that was great for shopping for food and bits and pieces. I'd go up there a few times a week, wheeling the pram with the babies in it, and buy bits and pieces for the house and for dinner.

As well as food shopping, it was a good place for a social catch up too. Now I wasn't too big on having a big social circle. A few friends was all I needed, who I could just have a chat with from time to time. Other than that I was more one who kept myself to spending time at home and with the family. But you do need those few females in your life to compare notes with, and this was one of those times. So that day I started complaining to one of my friends down there, and telling her I didn't know what to do about these bloomin' barber's trips, and that I wasn't ready for another baby just yet, but I couldn't rely on Charlie to always be prepared. And just like that, out of the blue, she started laughing.

'Haven't you seen Mrs Winky who sells the ribbon over there on the market?' she asked.

'No,' I said, confused.

'Well, she's always got a black pinny on, and whenever you see her, have half a crown in your hand ready, and just give her a wink.'

'Yeah, but then what happens?'

'She'll sell you some condoms.'

'No!'

'Yes, she will, I promise you!'

My God, when I think about it now, it's terrible this

is what we had to do. At the time I didn't really believe her, but I thought I'll just do it for a laugh and see what happens – I needed to take a risk. I was tired of telling Charlie he needed his hair cut all the time.

So the next day, down I went to the market again, and I got my half a crown in my hand and went to her stall. And sure enough there's this woman in this black pinny, and as I hand my money over I went 'wink wink' with my eye.

'Ok girl, one minute,' she says matter-of-factly, and she undoes her pinny and gets these condoms out. 'Here darlin,' put them away quick,' and that was it, sorted.

She sold ribbon, hair clips, combs and brushes and all that . . . and condoms! It was hilarious really.

Then I went home and I showed them to Charlie and said, 'Look what I got down the market.' He took one look, chuckled, and just asked, 'Are they alright?'

'Yeah, they're fine' I said.

'You can get them every week then,' he told me.

Oh, I'd shot myself in the foot. I tried saying, 'No, it's up to you to buy them!' but after that every week I went to her. It was probably for the better really, 'cause that way I didn't have to worry that he'd forget to get them and I'd end up with another baby before I was ready.

I used to tell everyone else about Mrs Winky, and

get them to go to her. Goodness knows how many unwanted pregnancies that woman prevented. She deserved a medal is the God's honest truth.

Years later my eldest daughter June used to go and see her too, 'cause can you believe she was still there, selling away. And I'd joke to her not to blink twice, and I remember she said: 'Mum, what happens if someone goes with a nervous twitch or something? They'd come away with a handful!'

Honestly the laughs that has caused us, talking about Mrs Winky since. God knows what happened to her. The market's not there any more, at least not in its original form. They have built a modern new version there with houses and indoor shops, as far as I know. It's a shame 'cause the old one had been there since Victorian times, and would have seen a right lot happen on its stalls over the years. But I guess, like much of East London now, it's having to modernize itself.

But at the time it really was the only option to get our contraception. It's terrible isn't it. Today you can get condoms anywhere – sometimes for free, or even in machines in toilets. I was lucky that thanks to Mrs Winky, I was able to have a bit more control over the speed we were having our kids. Not that I didn't absolutely adore June and Susan, and I did have every intention of having a lot more kids. Just at a slower pace.

Maybe the fact my own family seemed so broken up and non-existent by then was one of the reasons I wanted lots of kids – to surround myself with a big happy family. It was like where my own family had failed, I was making my own new one, and surrounding myself with my kids who I loved to bits.

I *still* hadn't talked to Dad since my wedding day. I'd often thought about him, and wondered how he was getting on, and if he had found out about me and my life through mutual friends. Or if he just didn't care at all. Most of the time I hadn't let myself think about it too much, though, 'cause it was just upsetting. I was especially bothered that it was now three years on from the wedding, and yet he was still too stubborn to apologize, so he hadn't met his two granddaughters. As with most things that I couldn't see a way of solving, I put it out of my mind and just got on with it.

Then one day Charlie's mum was out in some pub or another, and she saw my dad. He was having a drink with his lady friend – they were still together. And the mum-in-law went over and spoke to him. She told him how I was, and that I still lived at their house.

She said he seemed quite shaken to have seen her, and got a bit emotional about it all, and was pleased to hear my news, telling her he might come and see me. We still had no phone in our house in them days, so it wasn't that he could call me. He had to come in person, or not at all.

Well, when she came home and told me, I didn't know what to think. I got all shaky and worried, and I was nervous 'cause I missed having a dad, but it had been such a long time, and there was such a lot of bad feeling. Besides I didn't want his mention of a visit to get my hopes up and then it come to nothing. So I tried to put it out of my head, and thought I'd just see what happened. Then if he did come over, it could only be a good surprise.

One afternoon a few weeks later it was a hot day and we had the front door open to let some air through. We got some lovely warm days in those summers. All there was was one of those children's safety gates across the door. Them days it was safe enough to do that – there was no risk of anyone coming in, so the little gate was just stopping June from toddling off.

You couldn't dare do that now 'cause the kids would no doubt find a way to climb over and run off, or someone might come and snatch them, or burgle the house. That way I thought she could play in the corridor and run up and down. But soon she came wandering through, pointing back towards the door.

And, sure enough, I went to the door and it was my dad stood there. I just burst out crying and he burst out crying. The poor kids didn't know what to make of it! They didn't know it was their granddad 'cause they had never met him before.

Well, he looked like his old self, although older and more lined, but that was only to be expected. And he came in and we talked – probably the most open and emotional chat we had ever had. And he said he was so sorry, and he wished he hadn't done everything he'd done when me and Charlie wanted to get married, and then not coming to the wedding. He said he really regretted that he hadn't been there on my wedding day and he had thought about it a lot since. And then I realized it was too long in the past to think about again or to hold any grudges over it. And I just said, 'Don't even go there, it doesn't matter now.' And we were friends after that.

It was a real shame it took so long, and I hate to think what would have happened if the mother-in-law hadn't bumped into him in the pub that day. I honestly don't think without that prompting that he would ever have made the attempt to make things up. Maybe he was too afraid of getting rejected by me, I don't know. But I really think that one chance meeting saved our relationship.

After that I couldn't have wished for a better father–daughter relationship with him. He was around our house all the time, and enjoyed playing granddad to June and Susan too. He was more relaxed and, I suppose, happy now. And he probably found it a lot less stressful being a granddad than a dad. I could see Bet had turned out to be good for him as well, and from this point onwards I started to warm more to her.

But even more incredibly, him and Charlie, who had been sworn enemies before, suddenly found a bond and got on really well. So well in fact that sometimes I felt a bit left out by the two of them! It was like my dad saw the two of us together with our children and realized he had been wrong to judge Charlie, and that in fact we were making a damn good go of being a good family. So he stopped criticizing him, and instead the things in them that I could see were similar came through, and they connected. They would even go to the pub together all the time and everyone would ask if they were brothers.

As for my brother, we made up soon after my wedding, but I can't say we ever went back to being really close. We always got on well and met up at family events and all that, and, in fact, he had three kids by then – two girls and a boy – and they got on well with my ones, so it was nice to let them play together. His girls were like the spit of mine, so when they were playing together people couldn't always tell who was who – I swear you'd think they were twins. But on the whole,

Tommy and I both got on with our own lives really. He was a hard worker and focused on his family life, and 'cause he wasn't just round the corner, it wasn't always so easy to see him.

He liked a drink too my brother – as did everyone them days! But he kept himself to himself, and wasn't as bothered about getting in with anybody. So being sociable, in the pub and all that, wasn't his thing, so he didn't join my dad and Charlie on any of their outings.

Going to the pub was like a man's hobby. The men would go most days at some point. Normally they'd come home from work, and then head to the pub, while the women stayed home and did the chores or looked after the kids. If they were tired, or had had a particularly hard day at work, they might stay in and sit on the sofa, and talk at you until they fell asleep sat there. But go to the pub is most probably what they would do.

But it was a different kind of drinking to today. Don't get me wrong, of course they got drunk, but mostly it was just a kind of nicely drunk, not the drunk to the point of being sick and passing out that I seem to see today. Partly I think it was 'cause of the opening hours. Pubs weren't open all day and then long into the night. Mainly they would open for a few hours around lunchtime, and then again for a few hours in the evening, although longer at the weekends. But I think it was also 'cause people didn't have enough money in them days to get that drunk. Although, as my husband used to say, you could go out and get drunk on a fiver. If he was feeling hard up, he would go to me, 'Got a fiver, dear? Help me out!'

And whether I did would depend on my mood. Mostly I'd do it just to get rid of him, and get a bit of peace at home to myself! Even if I just had three or four quid he could go out and get fairly drunk on that. I mean it would cost that for just one pint today.

EIGHTEEN

Warming the Cockles

When Susan was eighteen months old, we decided to try for another baby. Charlie was keen for a boy, and he thought odds meant that this time we would get one. And sure enough, the mother-in-law was soon tapping at her nose and I was getting fatter.

But this time there was to be no hospital help with the birth – I had to have the baby at home. After I'd had the second one, the doctors at Plaistow Maternity Hospital said, 'Right, next time it's in your house' – I think that was just the normal way to do it in those days. The first two in hospital, then assuming you'd had no problems, you were on your own – other than the help of a midwife, that is. So I started preparing to have the baby in Bray Drive.

A month before the baby was due, the hospital gave me a box to help get prepared. It had everything in it, all sterilized for you, like gloves, pads and a nightdress. You weren't to open it until the midwife arrived, in case it got infected.

I put it right up top on the wardrobe so the kids couldn't get near it, but June, being nosey, used to say, 'What's in that box, Mum?'

I tried to ignore the question at first hoping she'd forget about it, but then I came up with a better answer. 'Oh, that's a baby,' I used to say. 'So as soon as we open it up I'll let you know, and that's when the baby comes, but for now, you'd better not wake the baby at all.'

That ridiculous story worked a treat, can you believe? She and Susan fell for it and were in complete awe of that box. They were always so quiet after that for fear of waking the baby, so when I wanted any peace in my room I'd just point at the box and they'd shrink back and be like, 'We don't want to wake the baby!', and tiptoe out. I used the same story with the kids through all my home births. I wasn't a believer in the birds and the bees chat at an early age!

As I wasn't to go to hospital, this time when I started getting contractions – 21 September 1960 it were – my mum-in-law had to run over to Well-off Kate's place and ask her to phone for the midwife instead. The midwife had like a little surgery, I suppose you would call it, or place she was based, not far from our house, and she came round on her bike, with a basket with everything in it that she needed to help me. Then she got down the box from on top of the wardrobe, and opened that up for the first time and was able to use everything in there too. Unless something went wrong and she had to call a doctor, the midwife would just stay with you so many hours like, until you'd had the baby, then that was it. It was quite a different set-up to being in the hospital.

While Well-off Kate was calling the midwife for me, she also had to call my husband 'cause he was off having a drink in the pub. We knew which ones he mostly went to, so she rang around them until she found him, then she got him on the phone. 'Right, Charlie, Pat's in labour.'

Well-off Kate had a list on the wall by the phone of all useful numbers, and the pubs' numbers were high up on there. I wasn't the only one whose husband was more likely to be found in the pub than anywhere else. And in an emergency it was much quicker to ring round than run round them as they'd have had to do in the old days, such as to let my dad know when I was being born. Oh, she was a useful neighbour was Well-off Kate.

Course, once he heard I was in labour, it gave Charlie all the more reason to have a drink – celebrating the birth of his next kid, or wetting the baby's head, as they called it. But he had the sense to know he was needed at home. So what better solution than to bring the pub home with him? 'Right everyone, off to ours!'

Next thing I know Charlie is back at our flat with some beers and his friends from the pub. There's me laying upstairs pushing, while he's downstairs partying. But I couldn't complain. At least he'd come home. Not every husband in them days would have thought it was necessary.

And to be fair to Charlie, he didn't bring friends round that often after the pub. The odd time a couple would come back with him, and they'd have a few beers and a bit of a sing-song. But really at that time he did most of his socializing in the pub, and then kept the home as a place for family. The birth of a child was the exception.

I remember when the midwife got there she said to me, 'Do you want Charlie up here with you while you give birth?'

'Can you get him up here?' I asked. 'No. Well, there you go. No, just leave him where he is.'

Instead, I had my sisters-in-law in the room with me, 'cause they were young and knew what it was like. And my mother-in-law popped in and out too. But the midwife was very good – reassuring and direct, while making as little fuss as possible.

It was pretty straightforward again this time, to be

honest – I was beginning to feel like an old hand at giving birth. I remember lying on the bed, it was an old metal thing, and holding on to the iron bars above my head, and just pushing. And soon enough out came our third daughter, who was eight pounds, and we called her Carol. Charlie came up to see me, and I think he was a bit disappointed it was a girl again, but then he saw her, and I think he forgot about that, and was just happy to have a healthy child.

Then before the midwife left she told me not to get up for ten days, the same as what it was in hospital. But come on . . . when you have the kids . . . it's not like when you are in hospital when you have no choice. No, I think maybe I lay in bed for the rest of that day, and then that was it, I was back on my feet looking after the kids the next day.

This time I never went back to work. We decided we could live off Charlie's wages so I could stay at home full time. I was also able to pick up some family allowance by now as well. Eight shillings a week for my second child, and ten shillings for my third, and any others I had after that. Not like today – what is it, £20 a child? Nope, then ten bob a kid was your most. Not that I complained, I saw anything as a help.

It also meant I was able to spend more time with the girls, and really bond with them. They became like my little friends. I really did enjoy being a mum. I felt really close to my kids and genuinely enjoyed all the time I spent with them.

It was about this time that June started school – and I don't know which of us was more upset about it. She was starting at Tidal Basin School, near ours, but oh dear, she screamed the place down when I tried to take her that first day, and when we got to the gates she carried it on and really showed off. But I couldn't get angry at her 'cause I was just as upset at her going. It was like that for the first few days, but after a while she settled down and then it was alright and she did well.

I think we brought the kids up well, I'll say it myself. They were polite and respectful – although more to their dad than me! He was the one who disciplined them. Yeah, that was always Charlie's role.

If they were playing up I used to say, 'If you don't behave, God help you. Your father . . .' and that's all it took. They'd be like, 'Oh no. We'll be good, don't tell him!' and suddenly I'd have some little angels in front of me. It didn't half work a treat.

If I'm honest, though, this was a hard time in my life and in our marriage. On the one hand there were a lot of high points – we loved the kids, and one thing I can say about life with Charlie is there was always a lot of laughter. Even when things were tough, he knew how to make everyone have a good heartfelt laugh and bring a smile to everyone's faces.

But there were low points. When you're hard up and you've got no money, and you want things but you can't get them, and you know the kids need and want things, it's frustrating. I mean, today that's why people go and borrow money, I suppose. But then if you didn't have the money to pay for something, you just went without.

And I did struggle with Charlie's drinking around this time which seemed to be increasing – I think because the poor man was working all hours to try and get enough money. I was at home so he was the sole breadwinner, so I think when he got a moment to relax, he began to like his drink more and more. You have to remember I was still only twenty-five and he was thirty. We were still young to have the responsibility of a rapidly growing family. I didn't like the drinking, though, partly because it used up money, but also because it made him say things he later said he didn't mean.

He'd come home sometimes from a night in the pub – Friday or Saturday nights were the bigger drinking nights – and I'd say, 'Oh, drunk again?' and he'd call me different names, like 'you miserable old cow' or whatever. I'd shrug it off, knowing it was the drink talking, unless he said it in front of the kids, then it would upset me.

But the next day if I was still sulking about it, he'd say, 'What's the matter, girl? Ain't you talking to me?'

And I'd go, 'You came in last night and said . . .'

'Oh, I don't mean nothing. You know I don't mean anything by it.'

'Well, why did you say it then?'

And it was no good arguing about it, so you'd just lift yourself up and get on with it. But girls today wouldn't put up with it. They wouldn't stand half of what you stood in them days. These days it'd be like, 'I've had enough of him or her' and we'd probably have got divorced or something like that. Which I don't think is a good thing mind.

No, I would get over the things that annoyed me, and we'd move on and have a good day, a day of laughter that reminded you why you were with each other in the first place. We did have some good banter together, and he could make me laugh more than anyone. Which is what marriage is. Getting through the downs so you can enjoy the ups, not just running at the first hardship. And it paid off in the end, we had a really good run together.

But yeah, they were hard days. And another thing that sticks in my mind from this period as adding to it, was the cold winters. Them days the seasons did what they are supposed to do – like it was warm and sunny in the summer, and cold and snowy in the winter. But for some reason there were a few winters around this time that seemed 'specially cold. Like the cold really got inside you, and no matter what you did to get warm, it didn't really work.

I can remember one very, very bad winter we had when I had the three girls. Everyone was getting moany and whimpery about it – and not just the children.

The only room where you could get a little bit warm was the front room. Like at Bilberry House, we had an open fire, filled with coal, coke and tarry blocks. We didn't have heating in the bedrooms, and we just had blankets to sleep under – none of these thick feather-filled duvets like you get today. And it got to where there was no point even trying to get to sleep there, 'cause you would just lay shivering and turn into an ice block. And everyone was getting sick.

So, finally, the mother-in-law said she'd had enough. And she went and got her mattress and our mattress and laid them on the floor in the front room to create one big bed. And all six of us slept there in front of the fire, dressed up in several layers of clothes, keeping each other warm.

I think Charlie's sister Mary came around too to join our 'camp out'. She and her kids were round our house more than her own to be honest, generally. She'd come for a day, then just never go home. Her husband would come too, most of the time, or sometimes he'd stay at their home. I think they were just happier when they were at ours.

So this one winter, outside the snow was built up really high, higher than I've ever seen it, so that it was almost impossible to go outside. Each day Charlie would struggle out and get to work – he had to if he didn't want to lose his job. But the rest of us would stay huddled up inside the house. And we'd take it in turns to go outside to the shops and get the food, but that was the only thing you even tried to get out the front door for. Other than that you just stayed inside and tried to keep warm.

It was like that for a few weeks until the weather started to thaw again. And wow, that was a relief when the warmth started to come back. We did have really bad, bad winters them days, not like they are now.

You would really have to stock up on the tarry blocks when you could see the cold weather coming. They were seriously all that kept you alive. In fact in some people's case it may have saved their lives – if an old piece of health advice is to be believed.

Anybody who had whooping cough was told to sit by a fire with a tarry block burning on it, and breathe in the fumes or the smoke or whatever, with tar in it. Then the tar would get down into your lungs and throat and stick, and you'd get yourself better from it. That's what they used to say, anyway, who knows if it was bleedin' true or not!

Well, I never caught whooping cough thank goodness, but I did like sitting watching them tarry blocks burn. They sent off all these different coloured sparks, more interesting to watch than normal wood or coal. We burned all sorts of other things on the fire too. I mean hardly anything went in the binny – what we called the dustbin – 'cause everything pretty much went on the fire. You didn't have all the plastic and packaging that you do today, but things like the potato peelings, or paper bags, everything would go on the fire. You'd chuck anything on it that would help it keep burning.

You did have a little round black bin for other rubbish, but you never had much in it like. You'd leave it out once a week for the dustbin men and it would never be full. Plus you didn't have bin bags. It just went straight in this metal bin. Then the bin man would take the lid off, throw what was in there straight in the back of the cart and set it back down for you. Then you'd wash it out, and start the week over again. None of this complicated stuff today, where you have bags and bags of rubbish, and it all has to be sorted depending on what it is . . . I can't stand that.

One thing we weren't putting in the bin was napkins, or nappies. No, in them days napkins were made of cloth, like terry towelling, and you washed them and reused them. Not like today when you use them once and throw them away. And I'll tell you what, at times when the kids were little, I felt I was on permanent napkin-washing duty. I'd have two buckets going on the gas stove, one for boiling and one for cleaning. And there would be a constant stream of these nappies going through the process. Then, once cleaned, they would get chucked into the sink, and I'd run them through the mangle and dry them, and they'd be ready to go back on the babies.

Oh, it was one aspect of motherhood I properly hated, but 'cause of that, people started to develop tricks to get around it. Like I remember my mother-in-law teaching me to use this gauze inside the napkin. You'd buy a roll of the stuff, it was like this thick linen gauze, and you'd make a square out of it, and put it inside the napkin. So when the baby did its business, all you had to do was wrap that up and throw that away, to save staining the napkins. I suppose it was like an early version of today's disposable napkins. When I think of the things we used to do, oh dear.

*

It was around this time we got a car for the first time. They were becoming more common, and it was no longer seen as impossible to own one – move over Well-off Kate! Though you would never have dreamed of getting a new one or anything. But when we had three kids to get around the place for whatever reason, Charlie decided it was the right time, so we got one in the end.

I can't remember what car it was, but it was a German car, a funny ol' looking thing it was. One of the fellas my husband worked for at that time was German and owned it. I don't think Charlie paid him straight out for it or anything, I think it was just taken out of his wages for a while. It probably made it sound like less money that way. I can't imagine what we did pay in total, probably something like fifty quid, which obviously sounded a lot more in them days. More like £5,000 today.

I never learned to drive, though, it was Charlie took charge of that. I can't even drive today. I used to love walking, but more importantly by then I had the children, so I think it would have been impossible to learn. Could you imagine me having them hanging round my neck while I tried to drive? It just wouldn't have been practical.

People used to drink and drive all the time then. I don't think it was even illegal. If Charlie had had a few drinks and needed to go somewhere in the car, he wouldn't have thought twice about it. You never even dreamed you might hurt someone. I suppose the worst you might imagine is you would bump your car, which would have been annoying.

Charlie was working harder than ever at this time, bless him, to keep the money coming in for our ever-growing family. I can remember him having three jobs at a time at one point. He was working early morning for a butcher, going to the market and getting all their meat for him, then taking it around all the schools and everywhere that ordered it. Then he'd go off cabbing, driving a taxi, in the day, to earn a couple more bob. Then of an evening he'd do insurance. He'd go round people's houses for a mix of reasons. First he'd be going to people that were already customers, and on the books, to see them and get their money off them, 'cause they didn't have direct debits or anything like that in them days, you just paid at the door. Then at the same time he would knock on doors of people who weren't yet customers, and see if they wanted to sign up.

I think he enjoyed doing the work, I suppose it stretched his mind and allowed him to be sociable too, 'cause that was important to Charlie, to be sociable. He'd never have liked a job when he was sat alone, stuck with his own company to entertain him.

NINETEEN

A Little Miracle

By now we had moved the three girls to their own bedroom. When they were each young, they would sleep in a cot by the bed in our room, but as they got older, and stopped crying in the night, I tried to move them into their own room.

We did the third small bedroom up as theirs. It was only a small box room, but it was enough. The three girls slept top and bottom at first in the same bed, sleeping with their heads and feet at opposite ends. But they didn't half used to moan about it. 'Mum, her toes are in my face!' 'Mum, her feet stink!', all sorts of things. So then as they got older and we had a bit more money, we got them some bunk beds, and they slept in those instead.

It wasn't always easy to get them sleeping in their own room in the first place, though. More often than not we'd wake up in the night to find one or other of the girls clambering into our bed to join us. But slowly they got used to their own room, and in the end I think they all liked it and felt rather grown-up.

Then just as we got some peace back in our bedroom, well, you've guessed it, I got pregnant again! It used to be a joke amongst our neighbours that Charlie only had to as good as see my drawers hanging on the washing line and I'd get pregnant. That made me chuckle that did – and at times like this I started to think it was true!

And it's good proof the romance hadn't died. It had faded on some level, of course – well, it had to, we had a house to run, jobs to do, kids to feed. So Charlie couldn't afford to be buying me presents or any of those kinds of romantic gestures. But I did used to moan at him, 'You don't cuddle me like those two over there, look at them!' if we saw a couple out somewhere all cuddling and that. But he wasn't a big one for public displays of affection. He'd turn around and say, 'I love you and that's all there is to it.' And I'd feel better and know I was being daft – besides, he was forever kissing me when we were in private!

But anyway, a bit of a strange story happened around this pregnancy. For as we got news that one life was joining us – just before Christmas 1961 – we were pretty sure we had lost another. My mum-in-law had this dog, I can't even remember its name, or what type it was, or anything, but it was this kind of little mongrely thing, that we used to pet and look after and feed and the like. It was a friendly, docile creature and the kids liked playing with him.

But that December, it was a real snowy one as I remember, and one day the dog went out and never came back. He used to take hi'self off for walks so it wasn't unusual, but we imagined he must have got lost this time in the snow, or hit by a car or something, 'cause he never reappeared. My mum-in-law was a bit upset, but we just thought we were never gonna see him no more, and moved on. He had been a nice pet, but to be honest we had bigger things to think about. We had the kids and the future baby to concentrate on, and money to forever be thinking about.

And, of course, there was Christmas. Christmas obviously added a bit to our money strain, but it didn't mean we didn't enjoy it. Charlie would always manage to get hold of a real tree from somewhere or other, and we'd put bits of money aside for presents and buy them throughout the year, to make it easier. Little things here and there. And mostly the children had to share presents – like if we got a doll, it would be for the three girls to share between them. But they never asked for more – they thought the world of it. Then they'd get things like pyjamas each, or a book on top of that. No, me and

Charlie did what we could to make sure Christmases were special, and I think we succeeded.

Anyway, later in 1962 I started getting ready for another home birth in Bray Drive. The same box arrived, and went up on the wardrobe, the kids tiptoed around the new 'baby in the box', the same as before, and I, well, I got fatter!

I felt like I was a different shape this time, and much bigger than in the previous pregnancies, so I crossed my fingers that for Charlie's sake I was finally having the boy he kept going on about.

And on 3 September 1962 I went into labour same as usual, and the midwife was called, and I hung on to those same metal bars above the bed as I went through the same ol' routine.

But the strangest thing happened when I was in the middle of giving birth. I swear it was like a miracle – though I suppose anyone other than the people in the room that day will struggle to believe it, but it's true, I promise.

Just as I started going into labour, this nose appears up the stairs and starts peering up into my room. One of the kids looks out, and goes, 'Mum, we've got a stranger here. Look who's come back!'

Nine whole months since that dog had gone missing, no word of a lie. He was back and came in and laid down at the foot of the bed. He lay there as still and quiet as could be the whole time I was giving birth, and then once I had the baby, the dog just got up, looked around, and walked out, and we never ever seen him no more after that. To be quite honest with you I might have thought I'd taken a funny turn and imagined him or something but for all the other people there. To this day I still don't know if it was just a funny coincidence, or some kind of animal instinct. It was like he wanted to check that I gave birth alright, then once he was satisfied I had, he left and went back to whatever new life he had set up for himself. Bizarre, but true.

And that baby . . . Well, I'd been a big pregnant lady for a reason – it was a big baby that came out! A full-on ten pounds, and you know the size of me, I'm tiny. It felt at times the baby was almost as big as me!

This time Charlie had been adamant it had to be a boy. He loved the girls, no doubt about that, but we had three of them, and you know what men are like, he wanted a boy. And I suppose he was feeling pretty outnumbered at home, five females and him.

So when I gave birth to a boy he was over the moon. Course he was downstairs hosting one of his usual parties full of people who had been invited back from the pub, but it wasn't enough for everyone in our house to know he was having a son, the whole neighbourhood needed to know. So he went and got in the car to tell them.

I think he went all the way around Canning Town calling out the car window 'It's a boy!' to just about anyone who'd listen – and those who wouldn't as well.

Funnily enough, I remember saying to Charlie at the time, 'Well, do you want to call him Charlie?' 'cause there was still a tradition then to call one of your sons after their dad.

'No, nope,' he said all definite like. 'He's not a Charlie.'

I was surprised, but reckoned it was his choice, and we ended up calling him Stephen instead. But true enough, as Stephen has grown up he has been very different to his father – if that's what being a Charlie means! So I think it was the right decision.

Not long after Stephen was born, another new arrival came to the house, that I was also extremely relieved to receive – a washing machine. It was the first one I had owned, and wow, it was a relief to have it. The funny thing is, at the time I thought it was the greatest invention for making life easier, but compared with today's washing machines, it did hardly anything.

It was this great big thing made by Hoover, if I remember right, with a lid on top that you opened up, and inside it was this big sort of drum-type container. You attached a hose pipe to your tap and filled it with water. Then once it was plugged in, the water would boil up.

You'd put your washing inside it, and leave it there boiling in this water, while the machine jumbled away, agitating the clothes and getting them clean. And I have to say you got some lovely whites out of it. As well as a proper clean for all those napkins! Then when they were done you got this huge pair of wooden tongs, like giant tweezers, and pulled the washing out of the water, before rinsing it out by hand in the bath. Then in the top of the machine was a rubber wringer or mangle, so you still did that bit by hand too.

You had to do your whites first, though, 'cause there was no changing the water for each wash – coloured went in after and so on. By the end of a washing session to be honest the water wasn't the best, cleanest water in the world, but it was still a lot easier and efficient than it had been before.

It was about this time I think that we got some bad news about my old Aunt Rosie – you remember her – the one who sold the winkles and shrimps on the barra'? Well, bless her, even though she was getting on, she had still been doing her rounds every Sunday. 'Winkles and shrimps!' at the top of her voice, and everyone still going to her just the same, for their pints of this and that.

But one day we got word that she had been killed. Hit by a car as she did her round. I can't remember the exact details, but there was a right to-do about it. Oh, it was awful sad. She had been a very popular lady in the area and it wasn't nice to hear she was gone and in such a way. Looking back, it was characters like her that really gave the East End its unique way of being at that time. But when I was a child it was just normal for me. It was only years later that I found out not every place in the country had a barra' lady selling shellfish in pints. Boy did they miss out!

TWENTY

The Drunken Midwife

And almost as soon as Stephen had popped out . . . well, I don't even need to tell you, I was pregnant again. I don't think Mrs Winky can have been doing her job properly. And do you know what? Yet again the mother-in-law knew before I did. I swear I didn't need a pregnancy test with her. We were sat there, and it was only about two months after I'd had Stephen, and she just looked at me, tapped her nose, and said, 'You've got another one on the way my girl.'

'No, I ain't! I've just had Stephen!' I was shocked at the thought.

She just nodded and kept tapping her nose. And sure enough, the next week I realized I was a week late with my period, and I went to the doctor's and he confirmed it. Ain't it funny how she knew, but there was just no denying it after that – obviously there's something that changes on your nose, though I've no idea what, no matter how much I've tried to look at it. Odd.

Once again Charlie was over the moon. He reckoned this one was a boy again, and so did I – 'cause I was so big again. I really do think I spent more of my twenties waddling around with a huge belly while I juggled a bunch of other kids, than I spent it slim. It was fine, though. I did like being a mother. I liked watching the kids grow up and develop characters, turning into real little people.

By now June was aged seven, and had become a real caring and helpful young girl. She would help me out with the other kids, giving them a bottle when they needed. Susan, who was five, was more unsure of herself, and tended to stick close to me or her sister.

Then there was Carol, who was two, and still in napkins, but already developing an independence. Oh, little Carol could be a handful at times!

Even Stephen, who was eleven months, was developing his own personality as quite a calm baby, although so far bringing him up had been no different to the girls. It almost lulled me into a false sense of security about giving birth again. But I swear, this next birth was one of the most ridiculous and traumatic times of my life. I can laugh about it now, but at the time . . . If I'd have had the energy I'd have killed my Charlie, for he really was inconsiderate that day.

The night this one was born, of course the same thing happened as with every birth – as soon as Charlie had news via Well-off Kate that I was going into labour, he came back to the house with all his friends from the pub, and a big party began going on downstairs. I always wished they'd wait a bit, 'cause they were celebrating the baby who at that point was still inside me just as my hard work was beginning. But no, they would get that welcome party going at the first opportunity . . .

So I was lying on the bed having contractions like, waiting for the midwife to come, 'cause she was called at the same time as Charlie. I had my four kids around me, sat on the bed and lying on the pillow beside me. They were sat with me 'cause there was no one else to look after them. I think by a bad coincidence, my sisters-in-law weren't around and the mother-in-law was out. Bless the kids, they had no idea what was going on, and I kept having to comfort Stephen, who was screaming for attention, in between dealing with the contractions getting stronger.

Anyhow, in those days the midwife would come on her bike, but I was halfway through giving birth when she arrived, with no word of what had taken her so long.

I'm there pushing, going 'there there' to Stephen, and just trying to keep myself conscious through the pain of it all. I remember June all concerned like, kept saying to me, 'Mummy, are you ok? There's a baby coming out of you. Mummy?'

Then the midwife arrives, just in time that she could see enough to tell that it was a boy. So she said, 'I'll just run downstairs and tell them it's another boy. Charlie will be pleased! I won't be a minute.' And she's gone. And that's it. She didn't come back. So I finished giving birth on my own until finally she reappeared just as I'm getting my new baby out and on to my chest. Who may I also add, was a whopping ten pounds eight ounces. Dealt with by me, on my own.

So where had the midwife been? Well, they'd only gone and got her drunk downstairs, hadn't they. I remember her clear as day, standing there at the end of the bed with a drink in her hand, swaying. And she looked me up and down, and said, 'That'll be alright, all that stuff'll flush down the loo and you'll be fine. Stand up and go to the toilet and get rid of whatever's left.' And I swear she turned and just sloshed her way back downstairs with her drink in her hand and her sashaying hips.

I was too exhausted to even be angry, and I just laid back on the bed and I went all woozy and passed out. The last thing I remember was hearing singing from downstairs, Charlie's voice the loudest, 'It's a baby boy, oh, it's another baby boy . . .'

The midwife was so drunk she apparently wasn't even able to cycle home when she did leave, and had to come back and get her bike the next day.

Can you imagine that happening these days. The midwife would probably be struck off, and the husband finding himself with a divorce on his hands. But as with everything then, well, you just dealt with it. You didn't always like the way things were, but it's how they went and that was that.

And believe me, getting pregnant never happened no more after that, don't you worry. I just thought, 'yeah, that's it, you ain't getting any more mate after that behaviour!' And I stuck to my promise.

But it was fine, Charlie accepted that. I think he realized five was enough for us too.

Anyway, whether it was knowing it was his last chance, or whether there was something different that Charlie saw in this baby's behaviour, he had a different opinion on this one's name.

'Name him Charlie, he's definitely a Charlie,' he said.

So we did. And they became Big Charlie and Little Charlie. Or sometimes Big Charlie and my little soldier boy. I sometimes called him that. I forget why, maybe because he was a tough little fighter. He was a rascal that youngest son of mine. I still call him Little Charlie now, although goodness knows why, when he is anything but!

Years later when we were looking back on that time, Big Charlie used to say to me, 'What you went through my girl', with this sympathetic look on his face. I can still see it now.

I used to go, 'Yeah, I know, I've got through it now, so don't start.'

'No, no, I'm only saying that what you went through my girl . . .'

And I'd cut him off, and go, 'I know, I know, but forget about it now.'

I couldn't be bothered with listening to it, when I'd gone through it all by then. But I was secretly pleased to hear it 'cause I knew it was his way of kind of apologizing, or at least acknowledging what I'd gone through with all them pregnancies. It was pretty late on to hear it, but better than nothing!

So there I was with four kids at home, and just June in school, but that only lasted for about a month before Susan started at school as well. Luckily, 'cause four kids to keep an eye on of a day was quite a handful.

Susan was just as bad to get to school in the beginning as June, the main reason being her bottle. She used to have a bottle of milk all the time did Susan, that she loved carrying around with her, so the idea of going to school and having to be without it terrified her. So daft as this sounds, every day at eleven o'clock I would have to make her up a bottle of milk and go round to the school and stand near the railings. 'Oi, Susan, over 'ere!' and she'd run over from playing and come and take the bottle through the railings and slurp the whole thing then and there. She was getting on, and not a baby any more, but she loved her bottle. And indulging it for a while was the only way I got her through those school gates.

TWENTY-ONE

Life and Laughter

Then Charlie's mum moved out. She swapped to a new smaller house with a fella she was courting at the time. I think she had taken just about all she could of our growing family, if I'm honest. She was getting older, and with five kids whizzing round the place, it was a lot to put up with.

We kept on in the house for a couple of months, just as family. It meant taking over the rent fully ourselves, though I think we were paying most of the twelve shillings and sixpence by then anyway.

I don't think the mother-in-law and the fella lasted long, but rather than move back in with us, so she moved in with Mary instead.

By then she wasn't in all that great health neither. She was diabetic, and in them days you didn't have the injections of insulin like you do now, you just had to be careful with what you were eating. And to be quite honest, she wasn't taking the care she should have, and was eating things she shouldn't have done. She was a big lady, and I don't think the diabetes and her eating habits were agreeing with one another.

But anyway, while she got on with life with Mary, I was getting on with life on my own in the house with five kids in the day. And I'll tell you what, it was near on impossible to get anything done. Imagine taking five kids that age around the shops for example. You would get nothing done, and probably lose one on the way!

So, bad though it might sound, with the mother-in-law not around to help out, I took to leaving them playing in the house, and running to the shop when I needed something, and getting everything as fast as I could before dashing back again. The shops were just a couple of streets away, and it is amazing how fast you can be when you need to.

June was eight by then, and quite sensible, so she was able to keep a bit of an eye on the baby while I did my dash. But I tell you, I did feel quite frantic at the time, and breathed a sigh of relief each time I got back to find them safe. But I couldn't see any other way to do it.

The local shops in Canning Town were pretty similar to the ones in Devons Road. Little local shops that each specialized in a certain kind of food. But I had a new favourite over here – Bacon Bill's. I forget the real name. But the owner was called Bill, and his shop only ever sold bacon and cheese, that was it. It was this big double shop, and I loved going in there. The kids did too when they were old enough that I could send them to run the errands instead.

'June,' I'd say. 'Run up to Bacon Bill's and get some bacon,' and off she'd trot, happy to have the responsibility.

Sometimes I did try and take all five kids out at one time, but as expected it always became a bit of a nightmare – even though they were quite well behaved, they were an adventurous lot.

The other nightmare was when it got to sickness season. Oh, I swear, every year, if it wasn't one thing, it was another. Whooping cough, measles, chicken pox . . . and once one of them had it, the lot of them did. Which, I suppose, was good, get it out the way in one go. But at the time it was happening, and I had five sick kids to tend to, each of them crying and moaning and needing something . . . oh, it wasn't fun.

Although at least around this time in 1965 or '66 Carol started at school too, so I had all three daughters heading off there each morning, and just the two boys at home. Unlike her two sisters, Carol didn't mind starting at school – in fact I think she thought it was quite the adventure and she trotted off happily into the building on the first day with barely a glance backwards. I was relieved, but also a little insulted if I'm honest! But that way I was able to look after the boys and not worry about the other three during the day. It was a lot easier, to tell the truth.

If we got away from the house, one of the favourite things they liked doing was going down to the train tracks to watch the old trains coming in and out of the docks. I think the lines that run there, alongside Victoria Dock Road, are part of the Docklands Light Railway now, or least some of them are. But then that didn't exist and it was all just for the docks.

So you had all these old steam-powered trains running along there filled with all sorts of goods. They were huge big old things, with coal or crates, or tins of food, and what have you on them. Anything really. I used to have a friend who lived along the road, and we'd call round on her, and the kids could play out the front and watch the trains while we kept an eye on them and tried to have a bit of a catch-up and a gossip at the same time.

Up until I had Charlie, I had just had a single buggy, as whatever kid wasn't in it was normally old enough to walk by then. But Stephen and Little Charlie were so close together in age that I needed a double one to fit them in – and any other of the kids that was too tired to walk as well. Well, I went and bought a second-hand buggy, I forget where from, but Brownie's honour I did! But for some reason my kids tell a different story.

Carol will always tell you this version, but I swear it's not true . . . I always go to her, 'What you talking about, I don't know what you're on about!'

She claims we went to the Post Office one day, me and the five kids and the single buggy. Then she reckons I said, 'Come on, jump in this buggy' and pointed at a double buggy that another mum had parked up outside while she was in the shop. And then we left with the new one, having abandoned the single buggy and nicked a double one.

Honest to God, though, that's not what happened. She always comes out with that story and I've no idea where she got it from. I'm only sharing it to prove the wind-ups I have to live with from my kids.

As well as the new buggy, life got easier thanks to my next new washing machine – this time a proper one, similar to the ones today, that really did do all the washing for you. Now that did ease my workload, which, as you can imagine, by then with all five kids was getting pretty high. Some weeks all it felt like I did was make breakfast, wash clothes, make lunch, wash clothes, make dinner, wash yet more clothes.

It was just a little cheap washing machine from some shop, but it was a good 'un. I'd snuck everything in it, and it would wash and rinse it all. I'd still use my mangle, though. Put it through, fold it, put it through again, fold it again. All until it was a tiny little square, then hang it out and fold it up, and put it away when dry. No need to iron 'cause the mangle had saved me that. See, not all the old inventions were bad 'uns!

Mostly, though, we only really left the house to go to the shops, or get the kids to school. The rest of the time I let them play in the garden or out the front of the house. Although they had to watch out for the annoying policeman, of course. He'd do what he could to make sure they weren't having too much fun if ever the kids were out there.

I remember one day one of the girls, I think it was June, had a bike, that she had got and taught herself to ride on. She was good, could almost do it as soon as she was on it. And she was driving it up and down outside on the pavement, just enjoying herself like, then next thing I know she came in to me crying her eyes out.

'Nosey Nobby told me off for riding my bike, he came out and said oi at me, and really had a go!'

'Well,' I said. 'Where was you riding it?'

'On the pavement, but then, well, I fell off the curb,

and on to the road, so I got into the road for a bit, but only a bit.'

Haha, I had to laugh. That copper was a pain, but the kids did set themselves up for it sometimes too.

Not that their dad laughed about it. When I told Charlie what had happened he said to June, 'I warned you about riding on the road, and of course you didn't listen.'

'But Dad, I fell off!'

'Don't lie to me girl, there'll be no more bike for you now.'

And with that he flung her bike out, and do you know what, she was the only one of the kids who got a bike, the rest of them weren't allowed one after that. Oh dear.

Around this time we were trying to save some money together. We didn't know what we were going to do with it yet, but we thought we should set some aside, maybe to buy our own house in the future, or for holidays or for anything really. But it made sense to set some aside each week from Charlie's wage when we could. It wasn't easy, and some weeks we didn't manage it, but me and Charlie were practical, we didn't need money to go spoiling ourselves or anything like that.

Then when Little Charlie got to being one year old, we decided maybe I could go back to work part time, to help add to this money. So back to Tate & Lyle I went again, although this time on shorter shifts. I did from five until nine in the evenings on a week day. So I could look after the kids in the day, get them to and from school, the ones who went, and see to the kids' dinner and that before I headed off to work to do my bit.

As far as how we worked out the money, well, it was Charlie who looked after it. I would use the money I had earned, and he'd add to that, maybe by doubling it, and that is what I'd use to buy things for the house, mainly the food.

Then if I needed more, say if the kids needed new clothes or something, I'd ask him for it. Don't get me wrong, he wasn't controlling it, I wasn't having to ask, like explain myself, and justify why I needed it or anything. And he never said no. It was just that it made more sense for him to look after it. Then he could use what he needed out of it as well, and put the rest away as savings.

Charlie always was better than me with money anyway. He was more sensible with it, he had more of a sense of what to do with it. I would get too easily swayed by the kids if they wanted something and buy it for them – only to realize later on that I had then run out because of it. When they started the whole 'Mum, can I have that, can I have those shoes' or whatever, as we walked through the market, I'd just give in rather than dealing with it if I had the money on me. So Charlie having control of the money stopped that happening too much.

TWENTY-TWO

New Dawn at The Rising Sun

As far as I was concerned, though, with the mother-in-law moving out, and us having the house to ourselves, that was how we were going to live for a while. But not so. Charlie had other plans. What actually happened was one night towards the end of 1967, Charlie came home and said, 'I might be buying a pub.'

Now he'd had a few drinks, and he often came home talking silly things after a night in the pub, and I'd have to ignore him. So I treated this the same, and just said, 'Yeah, I know, ok,' thinking I'll take no notice, you know. But he was persistent.

'No, I will,' he said. 'If the money goes alright, I might get a pub out of it. Matter of fact, even if it doesn't I think your dad might lend me the money.'

Now that annoyed me, 'cause while yes, we were getting on with my dad, I didn't want us borrowing money off him, I've never been big for that, and nor has he. We've always said you want something, you get it yourself, you don't start relying on other people to pay your way for you. And it's not good as far as I can see to go getting yourself indebted to someone when you don't need to. So I wasn't sure why he was talking like that.

'Don't even start,' I said to him. 'I don't want us borrowing money off people. We're managing, we can just about look after ourselves now.'

He just stood there repeating, 'No, no, no, no, no, no, no' and I thought what have I got myself into this conversation for, he's just drunk. And I put the whole thing out of my mind.

But a couple of days later he said to me, 'I want you to come and view this pub with me, called The Rising Sun.'

'What do I want to do that for?' I said, impatiently. 'Running a house is hard enough, I don't need to take on a pub thank you very much.'

But he insisted, and told me he needed me there with him to see it. So off we went to view this pub which was on St Leonards Street in Bromley-by-Bow. The whole time I thought I was just humouring him. I thought there was no way we were going to get a pub.

The Rising Sun was a place that he used to work in.

A couple of times a week he'd go down there and do a bit of cleaning or sorting the shelves and barrels out, and all that business.

Ironically, later on I found a photo of my dad and three of his brothers standing outside the pub getting ready to head off on one of their beanos. Strange to think that, years after, me and my husband were looking to buy the place.

So we went in, and can you believe, it was the first time I had ever properly set foot in a pub. Other than the hours and hours I had spent hanging around the entrance and corridor to the pubs with my dad, or making mad scurrying dashes into the bar before I was promptly thrown out, I had never been inside the main bit of the bar. And actually I was a bit intrigued. This was, after all, where my Charlie spent so much of his life. It was very ordinary inside, though. There was a row of stools at the counter, and a few little tables and chairs for people to sit at. The decor was pretty plain, and it had that smell that I later realized was in most pubs – like beer mixed with smoke.

This elderly lady was there to meet us. She was the landlady and she said that she wanted to give it up and sell it – I suppose she was ready to retire. But she said, 'I want Charlie to buy it 'cause I think he will make a good job of running it.'

And I remember I went behind the counter and looked at the pumps. As I say, I would never have gone drinking in one, let alone stood behind the counter in there and served.

And they were these old-fashioned pumps, with big long handles that you pulled down. And I was quite fascinated by them. And I imagined what it would be like working there, and I just laughed. I was the furthest thing you could get from an East End landlady. It wasn't me to be one of those larger-than-life characters you imagine them to be. I was just busy getting on with my own life. It wasn't me to stand chatting to crowds of men, handling the drunk ones, batting off the flirtatious ones, and cheering up the ones drowning their sorrows. Not that I totally understood at that point that a landlady does a lot of that.

Then we had a look upstairs, and I have to admit, that was the bit I did like. It was a much bigger living area than the house we were already in at the time over in Bray Drive. It had these beautiful great big rooms, and I worked out in my head that all the kids could have a bedroom each . . . Yeah, that was the one bit that nearly did turn my head to the pub that day. And, well, something certainly turned Charlie's head, although I imagine it was more something downstairs than up, and suddenly somehow it was decided that we were going to take it.

Charlie's argument was that all the kids were getting older – little Charlie was still only three for goodness' sake! But he wanted somewhere to turn his attention to. I couldn't argue that while I didn't quite see myself as a landlady, I knew he'd make a great landlord. He knew the pub business inside out, and what he didn't know, I knew he would make sure he learned. When Charlie wanted to understand something, he could be very focused about setting his mind to it. And of course he had the social abilities. He could chat to – and charm – just about anyone could Charlie. He knew exactly how to be a great host.

So before I knew it we were giving up our council house and moving to the pub. I can't remember how much we paid for it, but it was a fair old bit. We had saved some money by then, and so we were able to use our savings for it, but we did borrow some from the bank and some from my dad. I wasn't happy about that side of things, as I'd made clear my feelings about borrowing, and it was scary to tell the truth. What if it had gone wrong, and we got ourselves into bad debt? It was a risk. And imagine if we hadn't been able to pay my dad back? I'd have felt awful. But actually my dad was keen to be involved – I think he actually quite liked the idea that he'd helped us get the pub. Probably fancied that it would get him his fair share of free pints as interest! But we made an agreement with ourselves we would pay back both the loans as fast we could, so as not to keep in debt.

The kids had no idea what was happening really, but they loved the idea of moving. I think they just saw the whole thing as one big adventure.

Charlie's excitement about the pub nearly got him in serious trouble with me one night, though, in the weeks before we made the move.

Oh, this one awful night I sat up half the night in a right state. Basically, Charlie didn't come home. I remember sitting on the end of my bed, being really upset and crying my eyes out, long after pub-closing time was over, 'cause he just hadn't appeared. And the poor kids weren't quite sure what to do – I remember them sitting around me holding my hands.

It wasn't like today, when you could just ring someone's mobile and find out, or call a few of their mates to check everything was alright.

Oh, I had more tears than anything that night, but I just had to sit and wait.

In my head I was going, 'I wonder where he is, what he is doing. What if something has gone wrong, or he has had an accident?' And of course there is the niggling bit of you that questions if it's something else that's turned his head.

Well, when he did get home hours later, I didn't know whether to yell at him or cry. I think the state of me was enough to shock him, but he said, 'Stop being daft. You shouldn't have worried. I've been at The Rising Sun, and they were learning me how to run the pub.'

Who knows, I'm sure he was, but that evening I really felt terrible. But I could imagine he'd got all caught up in learning the ways of the pub – like I said before, when Charlie has turned his mind to something, he really gives it his all. And I trusted him, I'd married the man for goodness' sake. So I put that night out of my mind, and we packed up what we had – which to be honest wasn't a lot 'cause other than the beds, all the furniture in Bray Drive was my mother-in-law's, so we couldn't take that. Mostly it was just a few cases of clothes. I think we fitted everything we had in our car and moved it round to the pub that way – no need for a big removal van for us or anything.

When we got there the kids went mad running around the rooms, getting excited at all the space they had to play in. I remember standing watching and Charlie giving me a hug, 'Look at this, girl, it's all ours. This is going to be alright, I know it. More than alright!'

And actually, it was a good feeling. Just thirteen years

before, me and Charlie had started with absolutely nothing. Not a penny to our names, other than the few pounds I had hidden away that we had left over from our wedding.

Now we owned our own pub, had five beautiful kids that we supported ourselves, and a car, and we had achieved most of it on our own. It felt like we were succeeding. A new chapter in our life was starting, and right then, with Charlie by my side, I really felt like we could succeed at anything.

Recipe for Jellied Eels

This is a cheap, nutritious and filling meal. You can't consider yourself to be a proper East Ender if you haven't tried it – and loved it!

- It is really important that you make this with fresh eels. You need to start with them live. If you don't want to take them home live yourself – most people don't want to feel them wriggling around in the bag on the way home, or have to kill them themselves, me included – then buy them live but ask the fishmonger to kill them. If you say can he cut and clean them, this is what he will do: he will cut off the head, and slit the whole way down the body along their chest. Then he will scrape out all the blood and giblets and what have you from inside. Then he will give you them like that.

- Once you are home, cook with them that day to make the most of the freshness.

- Cut them into pieces along the body, about one inch thick and cut the tail off and get rid of that.

- Put the pieces to soak in salt water to get off any last bits of blood or insides.

- Then put them in a pan of water and bring to the boil. Turn it down and simmer for ten minutes. Or more importantly judge for yourself when they are ready. They should be just starting to fall apart a bit when you prod at them, or feel tender when you put a knife in. I suppose I just know when mine are ready – practise and you will work it out.

- Some people like to add other stuff at this point – onions, herbs, etc. But I prefer to keep it as pure and simple as possible, and just about the eels. If you want to add anything to your taste, this is the point to do it.

- Then make up some gelatine by adding gelatine powder to warm water. Eels have some kind of natural jelly in them that will mix with the gelatine to increase it, but adding gelatine too makes it better.

- Put the eel pieces in a bowl and pour the gelatine over them and put the bowl in the fridge. By the morning you will have jellied eels.

- You can eat them either hot or cold, but the best way is with mashed potato and liquor – a kind of green gravy made from parsley. Beautiful!

- If you want the eels stewed but not jellied, just boil them in salted water, without the gelatine.

ACKNOWLEDGEMENTS

Writing this book was great fun, but also hard work, and I had help from lots of lovely people along the way, who I want to thank from the bottom of my heart.

First off, of course, is my family. All my kids, grandkids, even my great grandkids, have been amazingly supportive. We are a close family, and always will be, and it's wonderful to know we always have each other to rely on. So a big thank you to all of them.

To my manager, Emma Rouse from Money Management, who patience and loyalty to me and my family has been fantastic, and whose hard work has made the last year so much easier. Thank you!

I would also like to thank Emma Donnan, who did a brilliant job of helping me get my memories onto paper.

To Ingrid Connell, Lorraine Green and the rest of

the team at Pan Macmillan for all their hard work on the book.

An finally to Claire Zolkwer and Gary Smith at ITV and all the producers at Lime Pictures for looking after me throughout my *TOWIE* journey.

PICTURE ACKNOWLEDGEMENTS

All photographs are from the author's private collection apart from:

Page 3, portrait of Clara Bow courtesy of Tracey Godden, Fern Street Settlement; children outside Fern Street Settlement © Harry Todd/Hulton Archive/Getty Images.